ROCKFORD
WRITES

COMPILED & EDITED BY
HEATH D. ALBERTS

DIGITAL NINJAS MEDIA, INC.

Library of Congress cataloging in publication data applied for.

ISBN-13: 978-1515340355
ISBN-10: 151534035X

FIRST EDITION – Published In The United States – 08/03/15

15   16   17   18   19 ❖ OV/RRD   10 9 8 7 6 5 4 3 2 1

For My Loving Wife,
Wanda Alberts,
For Her Tireless
Commitment To
Rockford's Residents

"If you want a happy ending, that depends,
of course, on where you stop your story."
Orson Welles

12

UNSOUND MIND

Kathi Kresol

13

"A sick thought can devour the body's flesh more than fever or consumption."
- Guy de Maupassant, *'Le Hora et autres contes fantastiques'*

"We are pained to be called upon to record a terrible and bloody tragedy which occurred yesterday at one and a half o'clock." These words begin the newspaper article that described the death of a young man named Banks Dixon. He was 36 years old, and he had moved from England to Rockford around 1854.

Life hadn't turned out quite the way Banks had planned. He owned a blacksmith shop with his brother in Rockford. He was married to a beautiful girl named Eliza Jane Lake. They had a little three year old boy named George, after Bank's brother. But then their life started to unravel.

According to the newspaper article, at first the only cloud on Banks' horizon was his father-in-law. Mr. Lake did not approve of Banks. In fact, in August 1868, he came to the house and took Eliza Jane and the Banks' son back to his home in Guilford. Banks soon tried to get his wife to reconcile, especially when he found out that she was pregnant with their second child. When that was not successful, he took drastic measures. Banks waited until Mr. Lake took his daughter on a visit to her doctor, and then went to the house and took his son back home with him.

Things got really ugly when Mr. Lake had papers drawn up for Banks to sign that would give Jane custody of George, turn over all of their property, and the sum of one thousand dollars. Banks didn't sign the papers. When he heard that Mr. Lake was coming to take his son, George, he left Rockford to go down south for the winter.

Banks couldn't stay away forever, though. He waited until Jane gave birth to their second son and then returned to Rockford.

Jane's life had not been going well since the separation either. First, she developed some kind of infection in her eyes. Then, after Banks "stole" their son away, she was always frightened. She became convinced that he would return to steal their second child and then kill her.

As her sight grew worse and her due date approached, Jane's father and mother moved her to Rockford. They settled her into the house of Mr. and Mrs. Worsley, and neighborhood women assisted Mrs. Worsley with Jane's care. Extra care was definitely needed, as Jane became almost blind, was severely depressed, and extremely paranoid. She had terrible headaches and was given laudanum and quinine for the pain. Mrs. Worsley testified that she would make mustard and camphor compresses to apply to Jane's head to ease the headaches. She did this so often, the heat blistered Jane's forehead and temples. After the birth of her second child, Jane took over five weeks to recover.

Upon his return to Rockford, Banks sent Jane a message that he would like to see her and their new son. He also asked her to reconsider a reconciliation. He wrote that if she came back, "he would do anything it took to make her happy if she would just return home." Jane agreed to see Banks, but her attending doctor ordered them to wait.

In the days that followed, Jane didn't seem as nervous as she had been. She was actually calmer, according to the ladies that cared for her. She even stated to the ladies who helped her each day that she was happy that Banks wanted to see his new son, and that she wanted the baby to look good for his first meeting with his father.

The meeting finally took place on May 26, 1869. By this time it had been around eight months since the estranged family had all been in one room. The family was not alone together, and the atmosphere was tense. Banks brought the lady who helped him with little George, while Jane had a couple of neighborhood ladies attending to her.

Eye witnesses would later say that Banks came in with Mrs. Luke, who was carrying little George. Banks crossed to the bed where the little baby was while Mrs. Luke took George to see his mother. Mrs. Luke asked George if he would go to his mother and kiss her. The little boy first said no, but Mrs. Luke noticed this seemed to anger Jane. So Mrs. Luke told the little boy to go to his mother and give her a kiss. The little boy relented, said hello, and kissed Jane.

They all sat down. Banks attempted to get Jane to talk to him, but she was unresponsive. He even tried to get her to shake hands, but she ignored his outstretched hand. Banks continued to try to get Jane to speak to him but, after a few minutes with no luck, he turned to Mrs. Luke and said it was time to go. He picked George up and took him to the bed where the younger boy lay. Banks mentioned to George that he should meet his baby brother and leaned over to allow the boy to kiss the baby.

As Banks bent over, Jane raised her hand and the ladies in the room were horrified to see that she was clutching a pistol. She fired two shots into Banks' back at point blank range. She was so close to him, in fact, that the muzzle flash started his coat on fire.

Banks dropped George, turned around, and wrestled with Jane for the gun. Banks then ran out of the room with Mrs. Luke following him, carrying George in one hand and trying to extinguish the flame on his coat with the other.

Banks made it as far as the back yard before he collapsed. Neighbors helped carry Banks back into the house, while the doctor was sent for. The very same doctor who had assisted in delivering Banks' second child

Upon arrival, the doctor found that the first shot had entered Banks' back by his shoulder blade and passed through his lung before settling in his chest. The second shot had entered his arm in the shoulder area, and the slug remained lodged there. The doctor announced that he could do nothing for Banks, and the poor man lingered for forty long, grueling minutes. For every second of those forty minutes, he struggled for each breath until he simply had no strength left.

In the meantime Jane was hysterical, crying and wailing about her babies. Nothing could get through to her until she asked one of the neighbors what was to become of her children. The woman turned to Jane and opined that she should have considered that *before* she shot Banks.

Jane was arrested, and charged with the first degree murder of her husband. Astonishingly, no one really thought that she would be convicted. A parade of doctors, who treated her before and after the shooting, all testified that she was suffering from depression. Further, she exhibited an acute paranoia that Banks was going to steal her second son as he had her first. This, in their professional opinion, had caused her mind to finally snap, leading her to believe that she had no other means to protect herself and her child. The gun, it was reported, belonged to her father.

Jane told doctors that she was so convinced that Banks was going to break in, steal the child, and kill her that she felt that she had no choice but to kill him first. Jane was examined by a pair of 'alienists' (as psychiatrists were known at the time). The trial was delayed several times due to Jane's physical and mental condition.

Banks Dixon was buried in Cedar Bluff Cemetery in an unmarked grave.

In February of 1870, Jane was acquitted on the charges of first degree murder, due to her 'unsound' mind. The courtroom was packed with spectators who immediately began to applaud and cheer when the verdict was read. As much as people in Rockford had loved and respected Banks, they also could not come to believe that such a broken woman would have killed had she been in her right mind.

Even Banks's friend, Mrs. Luke, when asked about the 'not guilty' verdict of Eliza Jane, replied, "Banks always spoke on her (Jane's) behalf and I had never heard him speak one word against her, but always to the contrary."

In 1876, Jane changed her last name, and the name of the two boys, George and Frederick, to Lake. In the 1880 census, Eliza and the boys are living with her parents. George is then called 'Phillip G.' and Frederick is then 'John F.'.

Jane inherited the farm in Guilford when her father became too ill to live there on his own. She continued to live there until her death in 1910. She left everything to her sons when she passed away. It seems that the boys had grown up to be fine men.

Sources:

"Notice to Banks Dixon." 17 December 1868 *Winnebago Chief* (Rockford, IL): 4

"Murder Case." 27 January 1870 *Rockford Weekly Gazette* (Rockford, IL): 6

"Extra Edition-Murder Trial Complete." 1 February 1870 *Rockford Weekly Register Gazette* (Rockford, IL): 3

"The Trial of Eliza Dixon." 29 January 1870 *Rockford Weekly Register Gazette,* (Rockford, IL): 6

"Mrs. Dixon Acquitted." 3 February 1870 *Rockford Weekly Gazette* (Rockford, IL): 1

"Probate Notice." 10 March 1870 *Rockford Weekly Gazette* (Rockford, IL): 3

"Probate Notice." 12 July 1882 *Daily Register* (Rockford, IL): 3

"Mrs. Lake is No More." 14 March 1910 *Rockford Republic* (Rockford, IL)

Inaccessible

Karna Tecla

20

If I could reach across the room,
I'd touch the beauty of your face.

If I could see across the room,
I'd gaze into your hazel eyes.

If I could listen across the room,
I'd hear the melody of your voice.

If I could smell across the room,
I'd catch the heady aroma of your perfume.

If I could taste across the room,
I'd savor the flavor of your lips.

But here I sit,
This pathetic old man,
On this bench
By the stone fireplace.

And you
The socialite over there,
You are the center of all attention.

My shyness will not afford me
The chance to ever meet you.
So I sit – here – and dream of you.

22

SUPERHUMANS ANONYMOUS

HEATH D. ALBERTS

Saturday, May 14, 2022 - *Superhumans Anonymous*

"Please, let's all be seated so we may begin," the moderator cajoled.

A great deal of cajoling seemed necessary as the loose cluster of individuals orbited around one another, avoiding collision like wayward electrons seeking a single nucleus.

It was my first time attending a meeting, and I was still considering bolting before it became too overt and uncouth to do so. As I watched the oft-misunderstood detritus of humanity each taking a seat, I found myself pulled by some unknown gravity to the closest unoccupied chair before me. As I touched the back, preparing to sit, the young man in the seat adjacent pierced me with eyes that suggested I select another seat, lest I lose a much-loved appendage. To my own surprise, I consented to this unspoken, yet nonetheless forcible, demand. It was unnerving.

Perhaps, I mused, *it's a facet of his gift.*

Once the group was seated, I took note of the empty chairs on either side of the fellow. It was then that I made the presumption that I had unwittingly broken some unknown taboo that was otherwise adhered to by the more seasoned members of the group. It turned out that I was half-right.

The moderator was slight. She was dressed in a pencil-skirted suit. It was hued in a shade of green that made her resemble a bipedal blade of grass. Her skin was hued in a delicate, flawless mahogany.

No, wait, that sounds stupid. I've been taking a correspondence course in creative writing in an attempt to reconnect with a more contemporary audience. All it's done for me, thus far, is to create odd juxtapositions in words and turns of phrase in what had been an otherwise normal lexicon up until that juncture in my life.

See?

I did it again.

Who *needs* all those words?

Please, just bear with me.

So, the moderator. What I should have said was that she was a thin and elegant woman, with dark skin, and eyes that demanded to be noticed. They were the sort of eyes that men for eons had killed other men over. And in this day and age, might result in some women doing the same as well.

"I see we have a new arrival to the group. Welcome!" the moderator announced, addressing the gathering but gesturing toward me. It was worth the embarrassment for the eye-on-eye action that accompanied it, even if it was only for a few fleeting seconds. Put those eyes on a big hirsute fellow, and I'd bet even-money that I'd still find myself entranced, enchanted, and unable to look away with any smidge of sensibility.

"Uh, yes, thank you. Hello," I replied, awkwardly rising to what was a ludicrous half-standing, half-hovering state.

"Please," the moderator added, saving me from myself, "you can remain seated. No need for formality here."

I gave an obliging nod, blushed, and rejoined my posterior to the foreign-butt-worn, padded cushion of the stackable chair. I'd have fired someone, during my tenure, if they had proffered a chair like this one.

"Would you like to go first?" the moderator asked of me. "Or would you prefer to get a feel for things?"

That question need not even have been asked. I still had myself convinced that I didn't know what I was doing here. Even at ninety, I was still recognized on occasion. "I think I'll just absorb for a bit, if it's all the same to everyone."

The moderator offered up a genial smile that intensified the effect of her eyes. I stifled the beginnings of a lump in my throat, whilst the remainder of the group remained stalwart in their indifference to all but themselves, and some to themselves as well.

"Well, then, I believe that we left off with Bill."

"We did," a snarky, twenty-something woman at my three o'clock added. "He was about to tell us just what in the hell brought him here."

"Yeah – *finally*," the teenager to my left (the one with the empty chairs on either side) sniped. "And, spoiler alert - it's a Duesey."

"Rory," the moderator interjected, voice taking on a stern tone for the first time, "what have we discussed about using our abilities in group?"

"I'm still not as annoying as your father," Rory shot back.

"Rory!" the moderator shrilled, wide-eyed.

"Sorry, sorry," the teen said, placating.

The old, scruffy fellow on my immediate left leaned toward my ear, and whispered, "Telepath."

"Ah," I replied. Great. The group had a telepath.

We're not all bad, came the voice of Rory, unbidden.

It took me a few seconds to realize that he hadn't actually spoken the words, and that no one else had heard him. I chose to ignore the mental indiscretion.

Bill looked like a naughty child who had been caught touching himself.

Not that that's ever happened to me, specifically.

"Well," he sighed, "Rory's not all wrong. Part of the reason that I'm here is that I haven't been able to cope with my...ability on my own."

"We're all listening, Bill," the soothing tone of the moderator offered. "And none of us is here to judge." Here, she none-too-covertly glanced in Rory's direction. "This is a safe place."

After a few additional moments of what I can only assume was careful consideration, Bill began to delve into his past in an effort to tether it to the here and now.

Don't Mess With Bill

"You see," Bill began, "I was in the Marine Corps. I was in the small ranks for about four months before I was pulled aside, run through a battery of tests, and then selected as an operative in a covert group."

"What sort of covert group?" the woman at my three o'clock interjected, clearly overwhelmed with intrigue.

"Loretta," the moderator responded, with the patience of a pre-school teacher, "please allow Bill to tell his story, his own way."

"Pffft," Loretta scoffed. "He'll leave out the good stuff. They always leave out the good stuff." It was here that she shot a look at Rory. It was a look that I couldn't quantify for certain, but I guessed what it meant just the same: *'Can I see you after group for some juicy clarification?'*

To his credit, Rory made no motion to reply. Then again, for all anyone knew he was belting out the second chorus to *The Battle Hymn of the Republic* in her skull even as I had the fleeting thought.

Bill plodded onward, "The group was selected, I soon learned, not for its military prowess, but for its physical compatibility with the experiment.

"The group was to serve as a bomb disposal unit, eliminating both conventional and nonconventional munitions in the field. The thrust of the —"

Rory failed to stifle a snicker. "Sorry, sorry."

"Right," Bill replied, before rethinking his wording. "The *main goal* of the experiment was to modify the human body to act as a dowsing rod of sorts. This way, we could walk into any area, locate, and disable any munitions that might prove hazardous to any and all troops who would follow. It also meant that no matter where we went, we could identify IED's before they had a chance to blow us to kingdom come."

While I listened to Bill, I kept a sidelong eye on Rory. A few of the words in the story seemed to drive him into fits of withheld laughter: 'impetus' and 'blow us' seemed to be the two main culprits. I had no idea where Bill's story was going, but this strange behavior had me curious.

"Certain promises were made, and certain briefings were held. Suffice it to say that I can't divulge a lot of this in-depth. I'm probably overstepping as it is." Here, Bill gave a lengthy and pensive pause.

"Bill, this is a safe place," the moderator interceded. "We've all signed non-disclosure agreements, and have agreed to be legally bound by them."

Bill had to know, as well as I, that those agreements were only as good as the people who engaged in them wished to make them. He also understood — as I did — that the putative damages outlined in the agreements were enough to make anyone second, third, and possibly fourth guess themselves before divulging anything. Assuming, that is, that the offender had anything of worth left to lose.

"Right. Even so, I'm going to skirt around most of the specifics."

"As is your right," the moderator agreed. "And I'm certain that we all respect that." This last bit was more a subtle demand than a statement, as her eyes shot a subconscious glance Loretta's way.

Heaving a sigh, Bill plodded on, "Our bodies were supposed to be infused with a bioluminescent capability, as well as a low-level muscle response. In English, that means we would glow when in the localized presence of explosives of any sort, and grow progressively brighter as we gained proximity. We would also feel a sort of...tug, I suppose, is the best word for it. Our whole body's musculature would feel compelled to move in the direction of the device." It was

28

here that Bill ceased speaking for quite some time.

The moderator asked, "Bill, would you care to finish, or shall we move on?"

"I...yes. I've held back through three sessions already, and I'm not helping anything by keeping this to myself."

"That's a very healthy observation, Bill. And well said."

"As crazy as it sounds, the experiment worked. The problem was, it didn't work as advertised." Again, a long pause ensued.

"How so, Bill?" the moderator gently prodded.

"Well, the bioluminescence was localized rather than entire. And the muscular pull tended to occur predominantly in those same localized areas."

"I see," the moderator offered.

"No, you really don't," Rory interjected. Then he winked at Bill and said, "It's all right. It's not your fault. Just tell them."

"Well," Bill began, "in me, the effects localized themselves in two distinct areas. Specifically, the heart, and the, uh, groin area."

Loretta's eyes glazed over, a golden yellow. She squinted at his midsection. "Seems all normal in there to me," she opined, "and impressive too, by the by."

"Loretta!" the moderator scolded. "Did we *not* just discuss this?"

"I know, I know. I'm sorry. But come on! If you had delving vision like mine, you can't tell me that you wouldn't have done the same."

"The point is that I don't have it, so there's no literal argument to be made."

This, to my way of thinking, was a non-denial denial.

"So what, uh, happens exactly?" the scruffy fellow on my left asked of Bill.

"Well," a crimson and chagrinned Bill replied. "When I'm in proximity, my heart begins to beat faster. A luminous, greenish-yellow glow is then emitted from my heart, and 'down there'. Priapism occurs, and then gets out of hand –"

"Seriously, Bill," said Rory, between uncontrollable fits of laughter, "I'm happy you're getting this off...your chest, but you need to choose your words with a little more care."

"Damn it," Bill half-hollered, "just let me finish!"

At which point Rory nearly passed out from the new wave of laughter that washed over him.

It was clear that the moderator was mentally scrambling to seek a solution to the conversational fallout, but she could not devise one before Bill continued.

"Anyway, priapism occurs - to the point of being painful. And if you make a 'four hours' joke, Rory, I swear to God I will punch you in the nuts."

"Now, now," the moderator interjected, "let's not devolve."

"I had that coming," Rory argued, once more winking in Bill's direction, regaining composure.

"So they run more tests than even the worst lab rat should not have to endure, in an attempt to determine why my wiener goes all compass and lights up like a glowing –"

"Dildo?" Loretta finished for him, snickering a bit.

"That's *it!*" Bill bellowed, standing bolt upright, seething and crimson.

I don't know why I did it, but I stood, too. I moved toward him, and embraced him in a gentle hug. It was my primal self, instinctually coming to the fore. I just wanted this poor, lost soul to feel like it was okay. To know it wasn't his fault.

And Then...

It was, I am told, a few minutes before I regained consciousness. I was lying prostrate on the floor. Above me hovered six other faces, including an ashen Bill.

"I'm so, so sorry," Bill offered. "It was just a reaction."

My current position, and the throbbing in my jaw, told me everything else I needed to know to form a cohesive picture of what had happened.

"It's all right," I offered, in truce. "I don't even know you. I had no right to invade your personal space like that. Still, the nuclear option shouldn't always be your first."

"It was a very kind, and well-meant gesture," the moderator added, as Bill heaved me to my feet, "but we all need to remember to respect personal space – mental and physical."

"I don't think he'll forget again," Loretta offered.

"Not likely, no," I agreed.

"I'm really, really sorry," Bill offered anew.

I could see that he meant it. "It's no big deal. I get it. Let's just move on."

As the group once more found their seats, I watched as Loretta leaned toward Bill, and loudly whispered, "I'd like to see that in action, if you're ever so inclined."

Rory's Story

"Rory," the moderator said, as everyone resumed the seats they had occupied before the hugging incident, "since you seem so chatty, why not tell us about your month?"

When I had first been informed of this group's existence, I had wondered how a support group could go a whole month between meetings and still be beneficial. Now, only twenty minutes into my first meeting, I was wondering how in the world that was enough time between them to prevent a non-premeditated homicide.

"Sure, fine," Rory scoffed, feigning an indifference that his body language disagreed with. "Mostly, it was more of the same."

Of course, everyone but me knew what this meant exactly. I could hypothesize a number of things in a matter of seconds. That being said, I was wholly unprepared for what Rory said next.

"I'm still lonely," he shared, sighing. "I've said it over and over again. Everyone who knows about my power calls it a gift. A gift!

"Me?

"It's something I wouldn't wish on anyone."

Once more, this seemed to be familiar territory for all involved. Once more, I was the odd man out. "If I could...?" I asked of the moderator.

"You wish to add something?"

"Well, no, not exactly. I just have —"

"He wants to know why I don't consider it a gift," Rory asked, on my behalf.

"Well, yes," I agreed.

"All right, you really want to know? Here's why: Captain Light Wanger there feels terrible for punching you, more so because of your advanced age.

"Lexi, whose name we're not supposed to know," here he pointed to the moderator, "thinks you're cartoon-adorable, but isn't sure about your life choices, given the fact that you just hugged a Marine you don't even know, and without warning. She also doesn't know why you're here, so she's wary."

I could see the rage simmering beneath the now-taut surface of

Lexi's features. The intrusion of his ability was one thing. The broadcasting of the results were quite another.

Rory continued, on a roll now, possessed, "Loretta is wondering where my parents went wrong, and hopes to God that a guy like me never gets within a thousand yards of her nieces.

"Gil has taken a shine to you, and thinks I'm a hoodlum without real feelings." A pause preceded a visible deflation. "I'm sorry, but you asked."

"I don't see how that –"

"It *does* answer your question, you dumb geezer! Imagine every girl you've ever seen across a room who made your heart, mind, or johnson do a barrel roll. Now imagine being able to know anything about them - everything. You walk over toward her and, unbidden, the singular attention you're paying her begins to result in psychic feedback. You learn that she's a slut, or you learn that she's cruel to armadillos, or that she likes spray cheese licked off of her feet in the bedroom. Any one of those things would be okay, so long as – for the entire time you were with her – you never *knew* them. People all have their dark corners. It's their remaining so, their having learned from the experience, that is a part of what makes them human.

"Even without those thoughts, imagine being able to ride along as a girl sizes you up as a man, as a potential mate. Every character flaw she notices, you know. Every cruel thought – no matter how unintentional – you are privy to."

Perhaps without meaning to, Rory had whipped himself into a frenzy of emotion. It was about then that he decided to hit me with a verbal sledgehammer.

"So tell me, you douche-canoe, how in the hell do I even begin to find love with all of those things working against me?

"Is that your idea of a gift; a blessing?"

"Let's take a quick break, shall we?" Lexi pleaded, as much as asked.

Intermission: >Insert *Muzak* Here<

"So," the scruffy fellow who had been sitting on my left began, offering his non-Styrofoam cup wielding hand, "are you enjoying your first session?"

I shook the proffered hand, and decided to give an honest answer, "It's not quite what I expected."

This seemed to take him by surprise. "Oh? And what did you expect?"

What had *I expected?*

It seemed such an innocuous question, but it was one which I found myself unable to answer. I deflated a bit, "I really don't know."

Satisfied, he gave a curt nod and a wry smile. "It's like that. The problem is, it's not like *AA*, or *NA*, or *OA*, or any of the other *A*'s. In those groups, everyone has the same problem. In this group, we all have the same generic *type* of problem. Sure it bonds us on some levels. But the issues don't superimpose as well.

"Know what I mean?"

I actually did. "That's a succinct way of putting it. I just suppose I figured that everyone would feel like me, or have come to this place in the same manner."

"Well lesson learned, hey?"

I smiled, sheepish, but thankful for the moment of companionship in this foreign place. "Lesson learned," I agreed.

"Name's Gil," the man offered. "In case you're wondering, I have issues with shockwave emanation. At least, that's what the men in the clean white coats call it."

"Is that a fancy way of saying that it's a farting thing?" I asked, joking. My sense of humor tended to lack a filter, and had never been my strong suit to begin with. Suffice it to say that growing up, my mother had always found herself in two perpetual states of being when it came to me: mortified and prepared to be so.

Even so, my riposte resulted in the desired chuckle from Gil. "No. Though that would put me in a position to give Bill and his genitalia a run for his money, wouldn't it?"

It was my turn to laugh. I was warming to Gil's simple charms, and it was heartening. I hadn't had a friend in a long time, and the feeling – while somewhat foreign, in a temporal sense – was washing positivity and comfort over me, "Especially if you ever became a couple."

Gil guffawed, almost spilling the remainder of his bitter coffee. "God, it's nice to have some fresh blood in this group."

"Unless one of us is a vampire," I countered.

"By my reckoning, that would have to be either Lexi who, for the record, is just a normal human social worker, or Jane. Everyone else, as you now know, is accounted for."

"What if I'm the vampire, though?"

"Well, are you?"

"No."

"Good. Because eating blood isn't a superhuman capability, so much as it's an unhealthy fetish."

"And still tweens everywhere want to get in on the action."

"It's a crazy world we live in."

"It's crazier with us in it."

"Touché."

"All right people," Lexi's voice said, piercing the localized susurrations of conversation, "let's resume."

Hot Group Action

"Who'd like to speak next?" Lexi asked, as the group did their level best to gain renewed comfort in the awkwardly designed chairs.

When no one leapt at the opportunity, I felt as though it was as good a time as any to indoctrinate myself into the motley bunch. I was still riding the high of human connection that I had experienced with Gil moments ago. In hindsight, I should have enjoyed that feeling a little longer rather than choosing that moment to begin baring my soul.

Hindsight can be a perverse mistress.

I raised my hand.

"Excellent!" a beaming Lexi exclaimed. "Please tell us whatever you feel comfortable with."

"Well," I began, "my name isn't important –"

"Wait, what? What do you mean it's not important?" Loretta shrieked.

"I mean that if none of you recognize me, then that's a bonus for me. If I tell you my name, though, then you're bound to connect the dots. And I don't know if I'm ready for that." I looked with stern intention at Rory.

His response was a subtle nod, which convinced me that he knew my name, but only insofar as he was capable of delving into my thoughts. His youth prevented him from making any further connections. His powers, however, would soon fill in all of the blanks, if he chose to permit them.

I had no doubt that he would, and no way to prevent this intrusion.

Jane, who sat to the right of Lexi in the eleven o'clock position, showed her first signs of group interaction by evincing a tugging smile and saying nothing.

If I were a betting man, I'd say that she was the only one in the group old enough to remember exactly who I was. Thankfully, Jane was also the most silent of the six social priests who would hear my confessions.

"My job would, on occasion, take me to places like the one which Bill described. This was a number of years ago, but even then those places existed. On one occasion, I was in an installation in Montana. While touring the facility, one of the scientists there attempted to kill me."

"That's awful!" Loretta cried.

"It was unexpected," I agreed. "Instead, when he activated the chamber, something within me changed. I could feel - well, not *feel*. I don't know how to describe the sensation, honestly. Suffice it to say that in the end, I could do this." I bit the figurative bullet, and permitted my hand to engulf itself in a skin of flame.

The group remained, as if frozen, gaping at my hand. Orange flames performed their chaotic ballet around my digits and palm. I simply chose to look on with them.

It was Rory who broached the silence. "Doesn't that hurt?"

I snapped my fingers, simultaneously shutting down the pyrotechnic display. The flames abated, revealing my age-spotted skin below. It was just as it had been before my little stunt. "No. And I can do that with my whole body, if I so choose. Or just parts of it. I can also hurl flames over a short distance, so long as I have something made of solid matter in my opposing hand to draw energy and materials from."

"That's so CB!" Rory exclaimed.

"CB?"

"It's short for 'comic book'," Jane explained. It was strange to hear her voice. We'd been in the same room for nigh on forty-five minutes, and I hadn't heard it before that moment. It was simple, yet bespoke an underlying intellect and sensuousness that I'd not identified in a long, long while. It was a voice that I was instantly desperate to hear more of.

"Ah," I replied, not knowing what else to say. "Yes, pyrotechnic characters have been around for as long as superheroes and villains, it would seem."

"It's just so weird to meet another CB," Gil opined. "I've been to a number of these groups, in a few major cities, and I've only ever met one other."

"Oh?" I said, curious.

"Yeah. He had elasticity issues. Mainly, he could jumble up his molecules and move like a human rubber band, bones and all. It did do a real number on his organs when he did so. Or so he claimed, anyway."

I nodded, considering, "I can see how your colon or heart might have something to grouse about, given those conditions."

"Ewww," Rory winced, at the mention of the colon. "Yeah, that'd be shit city. Like a human tube of toothpaste."

"All right," Lexi chimed in, attempting to restore order. "Let's give our newcomer a chance to continue speaking."

I had considered going into more depth, more detail. At that moment though, I felt more free – liberated – than I had in months. I had gained what I came for, and had no desire for more. Their acceptance was enough. Their shared plight was enough. Jane's voice, and the promise of working to niggle more of it out of her, was enough. She was the first woman who had intrigued me in any meaningful way since the passing of my dear wife, Joyce.

In summation. I was content.

"I'm good," I replied. "I feel better, just knowing that I'm accepted." It was the first time in a very long time that I was not seen as a villain, pulling the strings and levers from behind an occluding curtain. Society saw me as a monster not for my new-found abilities, but for my old ways and occupation. This, I hoped, was the dawning of a new me, a better me. At age ninety, I was running out of time for fresh starts.

Con Te Partiro

The group broke up shortly thereafter. Not wanting to seem too needy, I didn't hang around to see what human electrons jumped from atom to atom, nor what energy was released in doing so.

Perhaps if I had, I would have been better prepared for my second meeting.

"Was that Donald Rum–"

"Yep," Rory whispered, in a conspiratorial tone, to the inquiring party.

It was Jane.

38

RETURN TO FLIGHT

ZETHEN (BART LUHMAN)

40

While walking in a cornfield,
I stumbled upon a weathered kite.
Picking it up, the scars became apparent,
tarnished, broken supports, and missing string.

Taking it home, I fell in love with the kite's simplicity,
blue in color and speckled with green charms.
Unable to resist, my heart bonded to the repair,
desiring to return it to its maiden splendor.

Wiping away the blackness – may you feel whole again.
New reinforcements – may you take flight and never waiver.
Re-affixing a ribbon – may you feel connected to encouragement.

Venturing back to the cornfield,
a splendid kite returned to flight.
Rising into the clouds, it rose beyond my view.

MURDER AT WOLF GROVE

ERNIE FUHR

Nothing can be worse than the death of one's own child. But for Mrs. Bridget Hart, the circumstances made it worse - a *lot* worse. Her only two daughters were brutally murdered, at the hands of her oldest son. Six months later he would die as well, in a hangman's noose. Bridget couldn't lean on her husband for support because, two years prior to this, he had committed suicide. This is the true story of the Hart murders. It is a crime that is now largely forgotten, yet is still horrific, even 122 years later.

♦   ♦   ♦   ♦   ♦

In 1890, John Hart, Sr. was one of the most successful farmers in Winnebago County, with 240 acres to his name. He and his wife Bridget had raised a large family with eight children, comprised of six boys and two girls, Mary and Nellie. The Hart homestead was located six miles west of Rockford, near what is now the town of Winnebago, Illinois. Their farm was enclosed by a wooded area known as Wolf Grove, so named because it was populated with wolves and wild predators that were not uncommon in the days of the settlers. However, none of the creatures living in the area would be as dangerous as the one that would one day attack Mary and Nellie Hart.

In the winter of 1891, John Hart Sr., then 60 years old, wasn't feeling well. His non-specific physical illness led to full-blown winter depression. On New Year's Day of 1892, Hart ate a hearty breakfast with his family, and then politely excused himself from the table. He casually walked to the barn and mixed a concoction of Paris Green, a green-colored substance that farmers used commonly as a pesticide. Paris Green contained arsenic and was highly toxic, guaranteed to kill rats and bugs, as well as any man foolish enough to drink it, which is exactly what a despondent John Hart did on that cold New Year's morning. By nightfall, he was dead.

While John Hart's suicide surely affected his family emotionally, he did not leave them in a bad place financially. He left behind an estate valued at $50,000, the equivalent of $1.3M in today's money. In the spirit of self-reliance that farmers are so well known for, Bridget Hart and her children were determined to carry on with their successful family farm. After all, she knew that Pa would want them to. She also knew that she could count on seven of her eight children to pitch in and help her. Farming in the late 1890s, and on such a large scale, was hard work. Mrs. Hart took comfort in knowing that seven of her eight children were able-bodied enough to help meet the challenge. All of them except for the oldest.

In many families, the oldest son took on a greater share of responsibility and served as a role model for his younger siblings. But for John Hart Jr., this was certainly not the case. In many respects, he was considered a 'black sheep', having been absent from the family for 12 years, wandering around the country and drifting from job to job. This may not be uncommon for a young man but, in Hart's case, he hadn't left town on the best of terms:

"Hart was a bad fellow and was known as such long before he left Rockford 12 years ago. The statement that he had broken up a colored family and gone away with the wife has been made but the circumstances are not generally known. George Lewis, a well-known colored citizen of Pecatonica is the husband of the woman whom Hart enticed away. Hart took her to Chicago and lived with her several months, after which he deserted her."
(Rockford Daily Register Gazette, September 16, 1893)

During the 1880s, John Hart drifted out West, working at various construction and railroad jobs. When he wasn't working, he was in and out of hospitals, often for weeks at a time, suffering from malaria and venereal disease. Hart experienced many symptoms of syphilis, including abscesses, fever, headaches, and dizziness. He most likely contracted syphilis during his years out West, as the brothels did a thriving business servicing single male workers. While in Portland, Oregon, Hart was committed to a mental asylum. He later claimed that his friends had put him there.

Hart had worked for the railroad for five years when, one day, he fell from a railroad trestle, severely injuring his back. Hart's back injury meant a longer period of recuperation, ending his employment altogether. To cope with his aches and pains, he made regular trips to Hot Springs, Arkansas for treatment. He also used increasing amounts of morphine and laudanum, a liquid form of heroin which was legal and easily available. By the time Hart moved back to Rockford in 1892, he was ingesting 10 grains of morphine a day. While this amount wasn't strong enough to kill a horse, it was certainly strong enough to create an opium addiction.

46

Back on the home front in Rockford, Bridget Hart and her children carried on with the farm. Although the spring of 1892 was the first planting season without their father, they were determined to keep it prosperous.

The necessity of day-to-day chores surely helped them overcome their loss and grief. Farming 240 acres in the 1890s wasn't an easy job. There were no John Deere tractors or large equipment to work the fields; families didn't even have electricity, for that matter. Bridget was strengthened by her strong Catholic faith. She felt blessed to have five able-bodied sons to help her: Henry, Michael, Cornelius, William, and Daniel. The Hart boys probably didn't miss their absentee big brother, John Jr., nor think of him very often. He had been 'out of sight and out of mind' for twelve years. Even if John had been there, what would he have contributed?

The Harts had two beautiful daughters, Mary, 26, and Nellie, 23. Like many farmers' daughters, Mary and Nellie always did their part to help out. But they were also true ladies who carried themselves with a respectable air of class and refinement. Whenever the sisters left the farm in their carriage, they were clothed in beautiful silk dresses. Many people often mistook them as being twins. Mary and Nellie were active in St. Mary's Parish, and were very well-liked in the community.

In the spring of 1892, soon after John Hart Sr. had died and was still freshly buried, his estranged son John Hart Jr., now 34 years old, returned home to live with the family. By this time, John was a broken man, mentally, physically, and financially. One may wonder what sort of homecoming reception John got from his younger siblings because he was a much different person than when he left home twelve years prior. He sweated profusely, suffering from various aches, pains, and maladies. He complained of stomach trouble, headaches, and soreness in the joints. Occasionally, his skin broke out with lesions and he always had a noticeable scab on his head. Perhaps the change of pace and the fresh country air would be therapeutic for John Hart, along with an ever-ready supply of morphine, which he bought through the mail, from a druggist in Chicago.

Bridget Hart was a forgiving person. In her eyes, John Hart wasn't lazy. He did the best that he could, and was willing to make an effort to work around the farm as his health allowed. But his brothers had a different point of view; they often saw John sitting around the tool shed, complaining. He was usually too sick and weak to contribute much, especially when it was time to plow corn or bale hay. John's health perked up on only two occasions: when he felt like riding into town, or when he took a swig of laudanum from his 'medicine bottle'. Most of the time, they considered their big brother as nothing more than a pain in the rear end.

Perhaps the true reason that John Hart moved back to Rockford was financially motivated. His father, John Hart Sr., had left his family a $50,000 farm estate, but he had not written a legal will to make his specific wishes known. John Hart wanted his family to sell the farm, and he wanted his share of the proceeds. The rest of his family vehemently disagreed, particularly his sister Mary. There was absolutely no way that the Harts were going to liquidate their father's assets. After all, their farm was one of the most prosperous in the county. How would they support themselves without it? To their way of thinking, and most probably in truth, their oldest brother was not a rational person. More and more, he seemed to be downright crazy. That summer saw a number of arguments between John and his siblings. Nonetheless, John Hart kept pushing the matter, creating a great deal of strife and stress within the family. Mary Hart wasn't about to back down to this brute, even if he *was* her blood brother.

Some neighbors and relatives began to realize with renewed clarity that John Hart 'wasn't quite right'. Even in an isolated rural area, word got around surprisingly fast. John talked to himself constantly, which struck people as rather odd. Then there was the day that he charged out of the house, waving a large Indian blanket and shouting that he was, "chasing after the redskins". He'd gotten all the way past the barn before the girls, and some visiting neighbors, calmed him down enough to bring him back into the house. Agnes Hart, a family cousin, later recalled how, on the afternoon she came to visit, John jumped up and down on his bed, shouting like a madman.

John's family noticed that he hadn't been sleeping well. There were many nights when his constant pounding on the bedroom walls awakened them. Sometimes he hallucinated and heard voices. On days when John was really out of it, he would lapse into a delirium, babbling about being a fruit picker in California. As his mental condition deteriorated, John Hart behaved as though he were living in a whole different world, with no sense of the people around him. Later, when Bridget Hart observed that "John wasn't in his right mind since he moved back", she was putting it very politely, as any mother would. If the family and the community only knew the tragedy that lay ahead, they surely would have taken action.

Tuesday, September 5, 1893 delivered a beautiful summer afternoon. A light breeze blew across the wheat fields and through the trees on Wolf Grove Road. At the Hart farm, Mary and Nellie lounged in a chair and hammock in their front yard. Even on a lazy day like this, when they stayed home on the farm, the Hart sisters still looked radiant, clad in beautiful cotton dresses, their brunette hair neatly fastened with a ribbon. The girls looked up as the screen door smacked shut. Mrs. Hart came out of the house carrying a straw basket. She glanced at her girls, admiring their youth and beauty, at the same time wishing that they'd help her with the work in the garden.

"I'm going out to pick some potatoes and cucumbers for dinner," she said. *"Keep an eye on your brother. I believe he's having one of his spells."*

Mary and Nellie knew only too well what that meant: the empty, dark look in John's eyes had returned. A resurgence of the short, measured monotone in his voice. And when he spoke to them, the conversation would always drift back to one thing: his share of the inheritance.

If only there was a way to give John his share of the farm, they thought. *Maybe he'd move out once and for all and never bother them anymore.*

Good Lord, it had been a long summer in the Hart household!

Meanwhile, inside the barn, John stood in a dark corner and peered through a crack between the boards. He waited for their mother to be safely down the road, out of sight and out of earshot. As he watched his mother walk off into the distance, he took a small bottle out of his brown overalls and took a nip. Nothing like a little medicine to take the edge off.

John had just finished whipping up a fresh batch of Paris Green. As he stirred the deadly green substance, he thought about how the same stuff that killed Pa; about how something which brought so much pain to their family could also *help* his family by killing off all of their bugs and pests. He gingerly set the cup back on the workbench. There would be more pests to attend to.

John reached down into the pocket of his overalls and felt for his newest possession: a brand new .32 revolver that he'd recently purchased in town. He'd taken a little target practice with it in the fields out back, but nobody knew that he had it. Not even his mother. After living out West for twelve years, John Hart knew plenty about guns and how to use them.

Mary and Nellie were still in the front yard, laughing and gossiping like sisters often do. They were talking about their friend's wedding that they had just attended in town. They didn't notice John come out of the barn, approaching them from behind.

"Nellie can you give me a hand out in the barn? There is a leak in the granary and the oats are running out on the floor. We need to nail a board over it. Can you help me? You know my back is feeling poorly."

"Yes, of course," Nellie said. She hesitated and glanced over at her sister.

Mary returned an approving smile, as if to say, 'it's alright.'

Together, Nellie and her brother John made their way toward the barn. Once inside, John handed her a hammer and nails. *"Here, Nel. Now go on downstairs while I fetch a board from behind here. I'll be down in a minute,"* he told her.

Nellie slowly made her way down the dark narrow stairway that led down to the barn's basement, to the granary she would help her brother fix. It was a dirty, dusty little room and Nellie hoped this would be an easy job.

John came down behind her, whistling, carrying a board and wooden carpenter's box in his hands. John set down the carpenter's box and held the wooden board aloft, as if to size it up and make sure that it was nice and square. Then, with full brute force, he swung the board with all his might, catching Nellie with an uppercut across her jaw. In an instant, her body slammed against the wall like a lifeless rag doll. She spun around in a perverse pirouette. Before she could catch her balance, John lifted his boot and delivered a good swift kick to her groin. This sent Nellie tumbling onto the dirty cement floor. The next thing Nellie felt was both of John's hands around her neck, pulling her back up to her feet. And with the full weight of his body, he pushed her against the wall, her helpless arms pinioned behind her back. Nellie started to struggle and scream but as the scream left her mouth, John sucker-punched her in the gut and knocked the air right out of her.

John had Nellie's body firmly pinned. With one hand, wrapped in cheesecloth, he held her mouth partially open so that she couldn't scream or bite him. She whimpered and stared at John with a look of terror in her eyes. But John wasn't done with her yet. He clutched her head tighter. His eyes showed no mercy. *"Shut up! You little bitch!"* he said, through clenched teeth. With his other hand, John reached down into his carpenter's box and picked up a green glass bottle. But this wasn't a bottle of Coca-Cola that he was giving to Nellie. It was a bottle of their old family friend, Paris Green.

51

"Take this now, damn it!" And with that, John put the bottle up to Nellie's face and held her mouth open enough to force her to drink. He poured in the putrid green poison, until she started to gag. Without letting go, John allowed her a moment to catch her breath and then he regained his grip and jammed the bottle into her mouth again, emptying it of its contents.

It was like bottle-feeding an animal, he thought. *Only an animal is much more cooperative.*

When Nellie was finished swallowing, she started to cough and sputter anew. John stuffed cotton batting into her mouth and made a gag so that she couldn't vomit it all back up. With a piece of baling twine, he tied it around Nellie's head to hold the cloth in place in her mouth, tying it off with a hasty square knot. Only then did he release Nellie's now limp body, letting her fall to the ground in a crumpled heap.

John walked a few feet away from where Nellie lay and pulled the .32 revolver from the pocket of his overalls. If the Paris Green didn't finish her off, a bullet surely would. He aimed the barrel at Nellie's torso and mercilessly fired one round into her.

Meanwhile, in the front yard, Mary Hart heard the pistol's report. John and Nellie had been in there for some time. Were they okay? Was that a gunshot she had heard? Was her mind playing tricks on her? Mary had always felt a very special, protective bond with her younger sister. At this moment, a sinister feeling crept over her.

"Nellie!" She called in vain. No sooner had the words left her lips, than a sole individual exited the barn. It was her brother, John. Even from a distance, he looked far more dirty and disheveled than when he had entered.

"John! Where's Nellie?" she called. She expected that her sister might come out behind him at any moment. But she didn't. Nor did

John answer her question. He just kept walking toward her, and the house, holding something in his hand.

Nellie Hart, 23 years old. In spite of being poisoned and shot, she lived long enough to identify Hart as the killer.

"John! Where's Nellie? Where's my sister? What did you do to her?" Again, there was no response. John increase the length of his strides, walking faster toward Mary. Now sensing the worst, she bolted, running toward the front porch. John paused long enough to put the pistol back into his pocket. Then he broke into a dead run, chasing after his fleeing sister.

By the time that Mary had made it through the front door and into their kitchen, John was charging, at her like a man possessed, and was gaining fast. Once inside the house, Mary grabbed the first useful thing that she could reach. In this instance, it was an old broom that was kept in the pantry. As John entered, she spun around and smacked him with it as hard as she could. Undeterred, he reached up and grabbed the utilitarian end of it. She pulled it free and frantically swung it at him some more. Unfortunately for Mary, when a maniac is trying to kill you, a broom is a piss-poor weapon with which to defend oneself. John was easily able to grab the broom away from her, throwing it across the room. He grabbed Mary's arm and pulled her towards him, but she kicked John in the crotch. He recoiled in pain and let go of his grip on her for an instant. With her free fist, Mary struck him on the head and shoulders. He grabbed her flailing arms and pulled her downward so that she couldn't get a solid shot at him. Then he hauled off and swung at Mary as hard as he possibly could. He landed a good square punch in her nose, but the brave girl didn't fall, and she didn't give up. She just kept coming after him, a fury of fists and fingernails. As the two of them struggled, John caught his breath.

This is taking too long, he thought to himself. He pulled the .32 from his side pocket and put it dead level with Mary's chest and fired. The shot spun her around. In agony she screamed, running toward the parlor. He ran towards her and fired again. This shot knocked her down and she stopped screaming. She staggered into the room and steadied herself, leaving a bloody handprint on the doorjamb. Then, with two bullets in her and with what little energy she had left, Mary ran back out the front door. A heavy trail of blood remained in her wake.

John caught up to her just as Mary collapsed by a lilac bush. She looked up at him one last time, this time expressionless, no fight left in her. John aimed his gun at his helpless sister, this time at point-blank range at her face. He fired twice. With each shot, Mary kicked. Then she lay still, a halo of blood splattered over the green grass.

John rushed back into the house and changed out of his bloody, dirty overalls and into a fresh pair of trousers. He had to move quickly. He knew that his brothers would be home; the younger ones from school and the older ones from their neighbor's farm where they had been working all afternoon. Mother would be returning from the garden any minute now.

When Bridget Hart returned from picking vegetables, all she saw of John was a trail of dust as he and his horse galloped away on Wolf Grove Road. He hadn't mentioned anything about going into town. There was an eerie silence as she set her basket down by the well. The girls had been sitting out front when she left earlier. Bridget surveyed the yard and saw one of Mary's dresses in the grass next to the lilac bush. Had it come loose from the clothesline? Good God! Was it Mary? Immediately, she dashed over to the crumpled heap that was once her daughter. Bridget Hart shrieked as she poked Mary's bloody, lifeless body, her daughter's dead, glassy eyes staring back at her. Bridget Hart let out a scream that could be heard for miles around. She fell to her knees and fainted.

Mary Hart, 26 years old. Hart shot her several times.

Cornelius 'Con' Hart was only 14 years old, but he became a man on that fateful day. He was walking home from school and was just about there when he saw his mother running towards him from their front yard. Instinctively, he raced to meet her.

She was frantic and hysterical. *"Con! Con!"* she screamed, *"Mary is dead! Oh my God your sister is dead! Where is Nellie!?"*

For a moment, time seemed to stop.

Together, they dashed to the front yard where Mary lay. He attempted to calm his hysterical mother, while at the same time comprehend what was happening. Con loved his sisters very much and now here was Mary, sprawled on the grass with blood streaming from a hole in her head, just like the deer they had shot last fall. Bridget Hart fell to her knees wailing, praying that Nellie would come running out and comfort her, hoping that this was all a bad dream. But Nellie was nowhere to be found.

Con grabbed her by the shoulders and tried to look her in the eye. "Ma, stay here, I'm gonna get help," he said.

Without hesitation, little Con ran to the stable and mounted his favorite horse. Then he rode as fast he could to his Uncle Connie's farm, which was a mile and a half away. Uncle Connie Hart was the boy's namesake and rightfully so, as he was someone whom the whole family looked up to. As Con rode away, he noticed that their other riding horse was not in the stable. And where was that crazy damned brother of his?

♦   ♦   ♦   ♦   ♦

Six miles away, in Rockford, John Hart rode his favorite colt to the hitching post at the corner of State and Kilburn. John had been riding bareback and the horse was coated in sweat. He dismounted and handed a dime to a boy standing nearby.

"Look after my horse, boy, and if I'm not back by nine o'clock, go ahead and put'er up in the barn overnight," he said.

Then, John cocked his hat and walked through the doors of Golden & McDowell's Dry Goods Store where he bought some writing paper, envelopes, and a couple of good cigars. It was a little past 4pm. For a man who had just killed his sisters, John Hart carried himself as nonchalantly as a country gentleman who was in town on business.

♦   ♦   ♦   ♦   ♦

Back in Winnebago, it didn't take long for word to get around of the horrific tragedy at the Hart place, where family and neighbors gathered in the front yard. Bridget Hart was hysterical. Her niece Ella Hart did her best to calm her and help find Nellie. The last place to look was the barn, and the two women went there with great apprehension, expecting the worst. There, on the floor of the barn, was Nellie, moaning, bleeding, and barely conscious. Bridget screamed again. They rushed to the injured girl and helped get her to her feet. As they carried her across the yard, onlookers gasped in horror.

Emma Miller, one of those present, later recalled:

"I first heard of the shooting about 4 o'clock. Connie Hart came over on horseback and told us. I went to the Hart place, a mile distant, with Mrs. Burns. A number of the family was there when I got there. I saw Mary in the front yard, face up and feet towards the

porch. We went through the house and saw blood spattered on the door cases and also on the porch. Then we went towards the barn and saw Nellie Hart in the doorway. Nellie had hold of the lower half of the front door; her brother Dan first reached her. With assistance, she walked to the house. Her waist and collar were covered with Paris Green. Her lips and nose were swollen and there were other marks in the corners of her mouth, appearing as if it had been forced open; there was also blood on her head and binding twine around her neck. They gave Nellie eggs and milk in the house; Nellie's white waist and brown skirt were taken off and she was put to bed. I remained until Dr. Helm came about 6 o'clock. I noticed manure all over Nellie's face and some on the side of her skirt."

(Rockford Morning Star, January 26, 1894)

Katherine Hart, a cousin, corroborated the story:

"I went to the place with Ellen Hart and saw Mary lying dead in the front yard. I was one of the first who noticed Nellie in the barn door. There was blood on her hands and face. There was something green on the right side of her waist, and her mouth was swollen and bruised. There was a string about her neck and manure was on her waist. She was conscious at that time, but said her stomach troubled her. I was there when Nellie died. I saw blood on the doors and front porch."

(Rockford Morning Star, January 26, 1894)

They brought Nellie into the parlor and laid her down. She was conscious and able to talk a little, but she was in grave condition. Slowly, the sinister effects of arsenic poisoning took control of her frail body. Nellie vomited until she could vomit no more, and her body writhed and convulsed in pain. They moved her into bed. The first doctor to attend to her, Dr. Helm did his best to get her stabilized, but he told family members that Nellie's outlook was grim.

Charles P. Taylor was cutting corn at Connie Hart's farm that afternoon when the family requested his urgent help.

Taylor later testified:

"I got to the place about 4:40 o'clock. Mrs. Burns, Ella Hart, Mrs. Bridget Hart and others were there. I saw Mary Hart's body under a

rose bush on the lawn. I saw bloodstains on the front door and porch, a print of a hand being on the door-case of the front door; I saw blood marks on the organ and south bedroom door; the blood was spattered. I first saw Nellie when the two girls were taking her into the kitchen; they placed her on the lounge; her clothing was covered with green stuff, manure, and dirt. She had on light summer clothes; her waist was smeared with the green stuff. As soon as I got there, I jumped off my horse and let it go. Went into the house and Nellie was complaining of pains in her stomach. Her mouth was swollen. I asked them to give me some salt and warm water. They got it and she took it. After taking more warm salt water, she threw up three wash basins full of green and red stuff. Two strands of binding twine were about Nellie's neck; William Hart took a knife and cut it off. I attended Nellie continuously. The discovery of the bullet wound on Nellie was made by William Hart about 10 o'clock that night. The doctor came downstairs and examined it. The wound was charred, bloody, and burned, the hole being as big as a pea. I found a bloody handkerchief under the manger covered with blood, and I delivered it to Officer Bertrand. Alex Parkinson was with me and showed me where it was. Parkinson found a gag in the barn and gave it to me. I stayed at the house until after the funeral. Nellie died at 2:10 o'clock on Wednesday, Sept. 6th."
(Rockford Morning Star, January 26, 1894)

The authorities were alerted immediately, but it took a while for the sheriff and the coroner to get to the Hart place because they were in Rockford, some six miles away from the crime scene. When Sheriff Joel Burbank and his officers arrived, they secured the area as best they could. Criminal investigation wasn't a science like it is now. As such, it was not uncommon for the crime scenes to be disturbed before authorities arrived. In this case, physical evidence had already been tampered with, as well-intentioned family members handed over John Hart's stained and discarded clothes that he'd changed out of, hours earlier. They had also found the Paris Green in the barn, complete with the cup and mixing stick. It was no mystery who the culprit was or whom they were looking for; it was a matter of where he was and how far he'd gotten by now. Sheriff Burbank dispatched a search party to the neighboring village of Pecatonica, which was a little farther east.

Even back in the horse and buggy days, long before police scanners, television, or the Internet, news of tragedies travelled surprisingly fast in a community. By now, the word on the street was that a terrible murder had taken place west of town earlier that afternoon, with the suspect still at large.

In Rockford, John Hart strolled across the State Street bridge and walked into Van Horne's restaurant for a bite to eat. The waiter that evening, Hedley Jones, came over to Hart's table and took his order for two sandwiches and a glass of milk. Little did Hart know that it would be his last meal as a free man.

Jones had not met Hart before but, as any good waiter does, he liked to make conversation with customers, exchanging information or a little gossip.

"Did you hear about the murder?" Jones asked.

"No. What murder?"

"The Hart girls, out in the country. West of here. Shot one of 'em dead as hell. Poisoned the other. She's alive, but they say she ain't gonna make it."

Hart just shook his head and didn't say anything.

"Tell you what, mister," Jones continued. "When they find the fella what did it...hangin's too good for him. They ought to skin him alive!" Jones said.

"Yes, that's so," Hart agreed with disinterest.

It was a little after 8pm when Hart left the restaurant and headed east on State Street. He decided to get a shave while he was in town because, after three days of beard growth, he was looking mighty scruffy. One of the faces in the crowd who passed John Hart that evening was John Rush, who noticed that Hart fit the description of the suspect whom police were looking for. Immediately, Rush notified Officer Erickson, a beat cop standing nearby. At 2nd street, Hart turned and started walking south, on his way to Harry Sperring's barbershop, three blocks away on Kishwaukee Avenue.

After such a busy day, a good shave would be relaxing, Hart thought to himself.

Little did Hart know that he was being followed.

"Can I get shaved?" Hart asked, as he entered the establishment.

"Sure, have a seat," Harry Sperring replied. Then, turning to his partner, he added, "Billy, get our friend lathered up."

"This is the easiest chair I've sat in for a long time," Hart said, as he settled in for his shave.

There was an awkward moment as Harry leaned forward and went about his work, his face and Hart's face only inches apart.

"You just started up here, didn't you?" Hart asked.

"Yes sir." Harry said, as he continued gently maneuvering the straight razor. "Where're you from?"

"Chicago," Hart replied.

Officer Erickson waited outside for a few minutes. He went into the shop as Harry was finishing up, applying aftershave to John Hart's face.

"Good evening Harry," Officer Erickson said.

Harry returned the greeting as he took the barber's cape off of his client.

Officer Erickson paused and looked at John Hart, then nodded to him, "What's your name, sir?"

"Wilson. James Wilson. I'm from Chicago. Been going back and forth for the last 15 years or so," Hart replied.

"Is that right? Well, we've had a bit of trouble in town this evening. I need you to come with me."

Hart looked down, fumbling for a dollar to give to Harry. "Well sure officer. I'll be glad to talk to you, or anybody. But what seems to be the trouble?"

"You know a fellow by the name of John Hart? He looks a lot like you."

"Reckon I never heard of him. Is there a problem?"

"Sir, you're wanted for a crime. We can do this the easy way or we can do it the hard way," Erickson suggested, this time more pointedly.

"A crime?" Hart scoffed. "Officer, you must be mistaken. But I'll go with you. I'd just as soon walk downtown as ride."

And with that, the two of them set out on foot for the police station. On the way, Hart stopped. He wanted to go back to the barbershop for a glass of water and to take some pills.

Officer Erickson would not allow it.

So Hart took swig from his laudanum bottle instead.

On their way to the police station, just as when they arrived, there were several citizens and officers who recognized him as being John Hart, the man suspected of murdering his sister that afternoon.

◆   ◆   ◆   ◆   ◆

Back at the Hart farm, Nellie was in bed. She was attended to by Dr. Helm and Dr. Richings. They continued to give her salt water in hopes that her body would continue purging the deadly poison that was slowly killing her. Poor Nellie had wretched and vomited all afternoon until there was nothing more left within her to come up. Her last night on earth would also be her most uncomfortable, as the poisonous arsenic crept through her veins and laid slow claim to her body. As Nellie grew weaker, the doctors knew that there was little more they could do. It was only a matter of time. A modest girl, Nellie had been reluctant to remove her clothing, even upon her deathbed. But when she finally relented, and did so, Dr. Richings discovered a bullet wound just below her breast. Miraculously, the bullet had not pierced her heart or any internal organs. It was a clean wound which had not bled a great deal. This was how it had gone undetected.

Sometimes, a tragedy can have a positive consequence. In Nellie Hart's case, it turned out to be a helpful thing that her death was caused by poisoning and not by a bullet. Her slow demise over the ensuing 24 hours had allowed her to remain conscious. Though she was weak, and barely able to talk, she was still alert enough to tell everybody exactly what had happened to her, and to her sister. At noon on the next day, September 6, as her life slipped away, Nellie Hart gave the following statement to doctors, friends, and family gathered at her bedside:

"My brother came to where my sister and I were sitting in the front yard. He said, 'Come down and help me fix the granary.' It was broke and the oats were leaking out. He wanted me to come and help him so I went down. I got down to the cow-yard. He gave me a hammer and nails. He told me to go down in the basement and he went back to where he left the medicine in the haymow and got whatever I suppose he used on me. Then I got down on the end of the steps and he got hold of me by the neck. Then he got the medicine. Then he put the medicine into me. It was in a bottle. It was a kind of liquid, kind of green, it seems to me. I don't know whether it was Paris Green or not. That is all I remember. Didn't see him have a revolver in his hand. While he was doing this, he said, 'Gosh darn you, take that!' That is all I remember. It was about 3:30 o'clock. I don't know whether I can get well or not. I know that the

doctors both say that I can't. And I understand and I believe that I cannot get well. I feel bad on account of my mother. Otherwise I would just as soon die from all the troubles we have had. At the foot of the stairs he grabbed me and pushed cotton batting into my mouth. He was my brother, John Hart."

"*X*" (signed) *Nellie F. Hart*

61

Shortly after making this statement, Nellie Hart lapsed into unconsciousness. Her breathing became shallower, her chest heaved, and by 2pm, she was gone. With her death, the charge would now be upgraded to double murder. Because Nellie survived long enough to talk about the attack, there could be absolutely no doubt as to who was responsible.

At the police station, John Hart could no longer claim a case of mistaken identity, or that he was 'James Wilson' of Chicago, because several officers present were able to identify him. Police found it odd that when Hart was told what had happened to his sisters, he did not respond in the way that a normal innocent person would have. Rather, Hart showed absolutely no emotion or sympathy for his sisters. He didn't express concern for his mother, nor did he have a sense of urgency to rush home to be with his family. Hart sat expressionless. His only reaction was to say that he had left his horse tied up on State Street. When police pressed Hart with further questions, he told them that when he had left home, both of his sisters were safe and sound in the front yard. When asked who could have committed such a heinous crime, he suggested that 'tramps' must have done it.

John Hart had an answer for everything. After he was arrested and officially charged, and throughout much of his trial, he continued to deny that he had killed his sisters. The evidence, however, suggested otherwise. When police searched Hart and removed his belongings, they found a .32 pistol with a bloodstain on the barrel and four empty chambers. It was no coincidence that this was the same number of times that his sisters were shot, or that the bullets matched in caliber. Hart also had a bloodstain on his shirtsleeve, which he claimed was paint. His brothers gladly turned over to the Sheriff John Hart's bloodstained trousers, which he had changed out of. They also identified it as the clothing that John Hart had been wearing when they had last seen him that morning.

Another of the personal effects police collected from John Hart was letterhead and an envelope from a pharmacy in Chicago, addressed to 'James Wilson'. The letter from the pharmacy stated that they did only wholesale business, and that to obtain the drugs he was seeking he should contact his local retail pharmacy. It is not certain what types of drugs that Hart was seeking. During the trial, there was speculation that he trying to get Paris Green in order to poison his whole family. Hart's explanation was that he was trying to purchase 'Spanish Fly', the legendary aphrodisiac used for, among other things, breeding horses.

Neither of these claims could be substantiated, but the fact that Hart was using a fake identity to buy drugs suggests that he had sinister motives.

In the days following Hart's arrest, the murder of Mary and Nellie Hart was the main topic of conversation in the area. Citizens were outraged. Tensions ran high as some 3,000 people watched the sister's funeral procession pass through downtown, on route to St. Mary's Cemetery. According to one account:

"Grave threats were spoken and many a clinched fist was shaken in the direction of the jail, and loud demands made for the person of John Hart."
(Rockford Morning Star, September 9, 1893)

There were credible reports of area farmers attempting to organize a lynch mob. The plan did not materialize. This was most likely due to lack of leadership and organization. As angry as these farmers were, they did not have a designated leader, nor a plan, to successfully storm the jail. As a precaution, Sheriff Joel Burbank increased security. He also made sure that his men were well-armed, should they have to repel any mob of would-be attackers. Further, Burbank deputized ten riflemen. These he stationed around the jail. He increased patrols in the northwestern part of the city, with orders to disperse any crowds who gathered. Sheriff Burbank also set up checkpoints on all roads leading from western Winnebago County to downtown.

John Hart remained unrepentant and unemotional while he was in captivity. Hart's cellmates looked out the jailhouse window as carriages transported Mary and Nellie to their graves. John Hart remained oblivious as he sat playing cards. He slept well at night.

When a reporter said that armed men were guarding the jail to prevent him from being lynched by an infuriated mob, Hart told the reporter to go away and let him sleep, that the vigilantes would never be successful.

"And with that, the man charged with a double murder rolled over in his bunk and was soon snoring like a Mississippi steamboat." (Rockford Morning Star, September 9, 1893)

63

John Hart's murder trial commenced on January 22, 1894 and would last for fourteen days. Twelve prominent men from across Winnebago County were chosen for the jury, nine of whom were farmers. No sooner had the jurors been selected than one of them, W.A. Daniels, had to be removed and replaced. This happened after he was overheard making the comment that Hart should be hanged.

There was a high level of public interest in the case, and the courtroom was packed. By one account, 1,000 citizens attended the trial each day. Some spectators brought their lunches into the courtroom so that they could eat without missing a single detail of testimony.

John Hart pleaded 'not guilty' by reason of insanity. For his defense, he hired a prominent local attorney, John C. Garver, to take his case. In order to pay Garver's retainer fee, John Hart liquidated his share of his father's estate, selling it to his mother and his brother, Henry, for $2,500. By selling his share of the farm, Hart undermined his insanity plea and bolstered the prosecution even before the trial began:

"If Hart is sane enough to transact business, he is sane enough to know the difference between right and wrong." (Chicago Daily Inter Ocean, January 5, 1894)

Over the course of the two week trial, a total of 81 witnesses were heard, 61 for the prosecution and 19 for the defense. This included family members, law enforcement officials, doctors, friends, neighbors, and community members who had interacted with John Hart when he came to town on the evening of the fateful day.

Nellie Hart's deathbed statement, in which she identified John Hart as their assailant, was irrefutable. In terms of physical evidence, the prosecution had an ironclad case to establish Hart's guilt. His brothers had turned over the bloody, soiled clothing that Hart had worn and discarded in the house before he fled. The unused Paris Green mixture and stirring stick were in the barn, as was the cotton gag that had been stuffed into Nellie's mouth. The .32 revolver that Hart had in his possession at the time he was arrested was introduced. There were two rounds in the pistol, and four empty chambers. This coincided the number of times that Mary and Nellie were shot. The bullets were a match in caliber. Given the type and multitude of such damning evidence, it would not be difficult to convince the jury that the Hart sisters were murdered by John Hart, and not by a wandering tramp as he had posited.

Prosecution would also need to demonstrate that John Hart was of sound mind and not insane, and that he committed the crime with malice. Again, this was not difficult. During the course of the trial, multiple witnesses agreed that John Hart wanted his siblings to break up the family farm, thereby permitting him to sell his share. It was well known that Hart harbored a great deal of anger towards his sisters and they that they had fought about the proposed sale frequently. Hart was particularly hateful towards his older sister Mary. Their brother, Henry Hart, testified that he had:

"...heard Hart say that he would kill his sister Mary."
(Rockford Daily Register Gazette, January 25, 1894).

Multiple witnesses, including siblings, stated that, in their opinion, John Hart was sane and not delusional at all; that he seemed quite normal and well aware of his actions. An insanity plea or a crime of passion can be discredited if there is a situation of premeditation and planning by the killer. It seemed to the prosecutor that John Hart had certainly considered his actions, with malice and forethought. He had taken his gun out to the barn with him. He had gone to the trouble of pre-mixing the Paris Green. He waited for his mother to leave the premises before luring Nellie into the barn to help him.

If anything, this crime was planned and coldly calculated. It was not the work of a madman in a state of rage or insanity.

Bridget Hart did the best she could on the stand, but became very emotional at times. Overall, she did not make a credible witness.

Because of the trauma that she had experienced on that awful day, it is possible that her mind had 'blocked out' certain things. As a result, Mrs. Hart was unable to remember basic facts and events. For example:

- She did not remember what day or time of year the crime occurred.
- She did not know the ages of her daughters.
- She was unable to correctly answer how many children she had.
- When the prosecution handed her a diagram of their farm and house, she was unable to verify things about the layout.

Mrs. Hart's testimony was more favorable to the defense. She maintained, quite vehemently, that John was not in his right mind, as a result of his chronic physical illnesses. She also claimed that John got along well with his sisters, and that they were kind with one another.

Hart's defense brought in an expert witness from Chicago, Dr. Richard Dewey, who specialized in criminal insanity. In the nineteenth century, the field of criminal psychiatry bordered on quackery, and it was not the science that it is today. All too often, 'experts', such as Dr. Dewey, made their diagnosis based on the shape, size, and contours of a person's head as well as other physical features (a 'science' known as Phrenology, developed by Franz Joseph Gall in 1796). After examining Hart for two hours, Dr. Dewey came to the professional conclusion that he was mentally impaired, suffering from syphilitic delusional insanity. He based this finding on the shape of Hart's head and facial features, as well as the fact that his left arm was five pounds stronger than his right arm.

Under cross examination, Dewey admitted that of the 7,000 patients he had examined, Hart's particular case was the first and only case that he had seen where untreated syphilis led to madness and murder. Dr. Dewey's credibility as a witness was eroded when he revealed that he charged $100 a day for his services as an expert witness, and that he made his living solely from testifying in civil and criminal cases. It did not go unnoticed that of all the doctors who had testified, the only one who believed that John Hart was insane was the one whom he had paid.

On the stand, John Hart denied any direct involvement in the slaying of his sisters. He simply said that he did not remember anything that day, from the morning of September 5th until he was arrested that evening. It was all a blur to him. Under cross examination he did admit that his sisters were in the yard when he left that afternoon. He spoke of his long and checkered work history out West, and of all the physical illnesses he suffered as a result. He was plagued with dizzy spells and ringing in his ears. According to his own testimony, while Hart was recuperating at home that summer, he became convinced that his sisters were trying to poison him. He said that he had overheard them talking about it several times. At one point he stated that he had suspected that there was Paris Green in a cake that they had recently made for him. Twice while John Hart was in jail he had cut himself. He stated that this was not an act of attempted suicide, but was done in order to get rid of blood which he believed had been tainted with poison. It was only after these bleedings, he said, that he felt better and healthier.

Closing arguments were made on Saturday, February 3, 1894. The prosecution argued that there was no room for a "compromise verdict" and that they needed to uphold the law. If the jury was convinced that John Hart murdered his sisters, which the evidence supported, then they must return a guilty verdict. Prosecutors took note of Hart's lack of remorse. He did not murder his sisters because he was insane and delusional, they said, but because he had a murderous desire to kill them. If he killed Mary and Nellie because he believed they were poisoning him, there was a great deal of planning, premeditation, and malice - not to mention the cruel way in which they were ultimately dispatched.

The prosecution also noted that everything else John Hart did in public that summer was done in a sane manner: he had examined his father's will, had hired a lawyer, had conducted business transactions, and, in order to establish an alibi, had remembered everything else he did when he came to town on the evening of September 5th.

It was certainly convenient for Hart that he could not remember *any* interactions that he had with his sisters prior to that. This is a good case of 'selective memory', but it is not the mind of an insane or irrational person.

The defense appealed to the mercy of the jury, hoping they would safeguard the legal rights of the prisoner. If there was reasonable doubt as to whether Hart had all his mental faculties, the only right thing to do was to acquit him and send him to an insane asylum for proper care and treatment. The defense reminded jurors that they did have this flexibility, and further that there was legal precedent for showing this discretion. In some last ditch arguments to buttress the insanity defense, Hart's lawyer claimed that because he hung around town and did not flee or escape by train, which any rational person would have done, he must be insane. They also noted that there was a history of insanity in the family, as Hart's father, aunt, and uncle all had serious mental problems. Incidentally, this argument was discredited during the trial, as two of the three insane relatives were an aunt and uncle back in Ireland who were only related by marriage.

The defense argued that John Hart did not have any quarrel or animosity towards his younger sister, Nellie. Accordingly, Nellie's deathbed statement did not directly criticize or condemn John. Rather, the dying girl was more concerned with the welfare of their poor mother, Bridget Hart. On that note, the defense hoped that the jury would also think of Bridget Hart as they deliberated, and show mercy on the surviving family members.

"God only knows better than that mother, the condition John Hart was in last summer. The sorrow that mother has endured has certainly been great. The atrocity of this crime has convinced me of the insanity of this defendant, and I ask you to temper your verdict with mercy. Don't send another arrow into the bleeding heart of this poor mother, and I shall be satisfied."
(Rockford Daily Register Gazette, February 3, 1894)

John Hart and his defense lawyer held out hope that the jury would have a reasonable doubt as to his sanity. The best outcome being that he would spend the rest of his life in an insane asylum. However, if Hart was found guilty of double homicide, he was eligible for a sentence ranging from fourteen years in the penitentiary to death.

At noon on Monday, February 5, 1894, after deliberating for a 1 ½ hours, the twelve jurors solemnly filed back into the courtroom with their verdict. The jury foreman, Robert Simpson, handed a slip of paper to the court clerk, who then handed it to Judge Shaw. The judge glanced at the verdict and gave a perfunctory nod to Simpson to proceed.

The air in the courtroom was thick with tension as Simpson turned to face the anxious courtroom. "We, the jury, find the defendant, John Hart, guilty of murder as charged in the indictment and place the punishment at the death penalty."

On March 16 1894, John Hart would hang by the neck until dead for the heinous crime of killing his two sisters.

From the very moment the sentence was handed down, until the day John Hart went to the gallows, he continued to keep his calm composure. In jail, Hart ate well and spent his final days reclining on his cot and enjoying cigars. On most nights he stayed up until 4am, reading in his cell. In statements Hart made to jailers or reporters, he continued to maintain his innocence while complaining that he hadn't gotten a fair trial. He loved his sisters, he said. Besides, if he were a vicious murderer, why would he come home to kill his family? After all, when he worked out West, he had plenty of opportunities to kill men who had thousands of dollars on them without getting caught.

Three days before his execution, John Hart granted a special interview to a reporter from the Rockford Morning Star. The two men conversed for three hours and Hart said very little that hadn't already been disclosed during the trial. He did, however, seem more sincere as he reflected on his terrible crime. While traveling and working out West, Hart had become very sick with a number of illnesses: malaria, syphilis, and a serious case of the 'grippe' (now commonly known as the flu):

"While I had the grippe, I was thrown into that condition which resulted in delusion. I got it into my head that my sisters were trying to poison me. They would always put sauce on the table at night but I would never eat any of it because I thought that they had poison in it...I believe it was the grip that diseased my mind. I believe that it put me in a delusionary state. I could hear voices in my head say, 'They are trying to poison me. Kill them. Kill them'."
(Rockford Morning Star, March 13, 1894)

John recalled how their mother, Bridget Hart, nursed him back to good health the first time he had returned home. But John Hart decided to go to Hot Springs for medical treatment, not only for his own well-being, but so that he wouldn't act upon his urges and resort to violence. Unfortunately, while Hart was in Hot Springs, he said that he "lost his mind entirely". Eventually, he was given permission to return home again, but with heavy medication. By the time Hart had returned home, he had contracted malaria once again, and he repeated the cycle of sickness, madness, and delusion. He often suffered headaches and tinnitus. Then, the familiar voices in his head returned, convincing Hart that his sisters were poisoning him when they served him breakfast.

The most telling moment of Hart's interview was when, for the first time, he conceded that he probably had killed his sisters. This is as close as Hart ever came to a confession, although he continued to cling to the insanity defense and insist that he didn't remember having done the deed:

"I do not remember poisoning or shooting them, but I have been told that I did both, and I suppose I did, but I cannot understand how I ever poisoned them. There were times when everything seemed like a dream, then I would get worked up to a nervous pitch, and reach a point where everything would become black, and I supposed it was at such a time that I committed the deed....All I can remember is that they were trying to take my life by poisoning, and I asked them why they did it on the afternoon of the tragedy. I cannot understand why I left them and did not think about or remember them until that fellow over at the restaurant had told me, and then I did not take any stock in his story."

(Rockford Morning Star, March 13, 1894)

Just as his Bridget Hart had testified during the trial, John Hart recalled vomiting a green substance one morning when he became violently ill. He put some of his green vomit in a little bottle and kept it under his pillow. If this claim were true, it would give validity to Hart's claim that he was being poisoned, and it may have strengthened his defense somewhat. But the obvious lack of physical evidence made it an incontrovertible point.

"I never had any desire to kill them when my mind was all right. If I had been able to reason correctly, I certainly would have taken that bottle of Paris Green that I vomited up to town to have it analyzed before I went as far as it is said that I did."

(Rockford Morning Star, March 13, 1894)

A public execution has to be performed properly, so that the condemned is dispatched as smoothly and efficiently as possible. Justice officials in Rockford shuddered at the thought of having a situation like the one that had only recently occurred in Chicago.

70

Specifically, two months prior, the execution of murderer George Painter had been badly botched. Instead of gracefully plunging to his death, the hanging rope broke and he tumbled to the concrete floor below, right onto his head. Painter most likely broke his neck the first time, but officials weren't completely sure, as he lay bleeding and unconscious under the gallows. They picked up his body and carried him back to the top of the scaffold, hoping to get it right the second time. It was a gruesome, unpleasant scenario for all parties involved.

Sheriff Joel Burbank took no pleasure in legally killing a man, yet he was determined to do his duty with both dignity and professionalism, leaving nothing to chance. He personally went to Chicago to select the instrument of execution. The rope that was used to hang John Hart was over a half-inch thick, made of Italian hemp, and specially constructed with an inner and outer coil. According to the Rockford Daily Register Gazette, this rope was "strong enough to hang a Clydesdale".

Incidentally, Hart's rope was cut from the very same strand that would be used four months later, when Patrick Prendergast, the man who assassinated Chicago Mayor Carter Harrison, went to the gallows.

Sheriff Burbank hired the services of Charles Cordie, a Chicago man considered to be an expert in conducting public hangings. For a modest $5 per diem, Cordie had supervised the construction of gallows all over Illinois and assisted officials on the appointed day. Under Cordie's supervision, a local carpenter named Reuben Cook built the gallows in Rockford from which John Hart would hang. A stockade enclosure was erected just outside the Winnebago County Jail, with a high fence to prevent too many onlookers and any unwanted audience participation. A stairway of seven steps led up to the 30' x 18' scaffold platform. The height from which Hart would drop was 8.5 feet off the ground. The law of gravity ensured that a fall of six feet was sufficient to get the job done on Hart, who weighed 230 pounds.

The old Winnebago County Courthouse.
A large crowd gathered to wait for the fatal drop.

71

The hanging of John Hart on March 16, 1894, was a macabre, community social event. An invitation and special tickets went out to 125 spectators, carefully selected to witness the actual hanging inside the stockade. Of the 125 invitees, only 75 people actually showed up. There were three rows of chairs for the media and members of the jury. Outside of the walls, the courthouse grounds took on a circus-like atmosphere, as some 1,500 residents turned out to attend Hart's execution. It had been 38 years since Rockford's last public hanging. On that March morning, the citizens hated John Hart every bit as much as they had hated the last hanging victim, the cattle rustler who had shot Sheriff John Taylor in 1856.

People from all walks of life anxiously strolled the grounds, talking, venting, and hoping to catch a glimpse of something. More than anything, they wanted the satisfaction of knowing that justice had been served.

On his last night on earth, John Hart got a clean shave and a fresh haircut, then spent the rest of the evening receiving friends and visitors. He left last minute instructions to his brothers that they take possession of all of his clothing and belongings, including the items of evidence that were used in the trial.

"If you don't," he said, "every relic hunter in Winnebago County will want a piece of them, saying they were worn by John Hart."

He was assigned three guards to watch over him. According to his watchers, John Hart was in a jovial mood all night, talking and joking. He spoke freely of the fate that awaited him the next day.

"So help me God, I know nothing of the crime I have been charged with. My mind is a complete blank on the subject. I am not afraid to meet God and I will die feeling that I am morally innocent of any crime."

After three hours of sleep, John Hart awoke in his cell and ate a hearty breakfast of steak and eggs with toast, followed by a good cigar. There would be one more important visitor to see him, Father Solon, who was the priest at St. Mary's in Rockford, where the Hart family were parishioners. Father Solon had spent a lot of time with the Hart family, and he would be with John Hart throughout this day. Nobody knows what Father Solon and John Hart talked about in his final hours. Most likely, the priest gave John Hart his last rites, as is customary for a condemned prisoner. He also probably heard Hart's confession, giving him one final chance to confess his sins and ask for mercy and forgiveness, so that he could leave Earth with a clear conscience.

Did Hart tell the priest that he had killed his sisters? We will never know. Church law strictly forbids any disclosure that breaks the seal of confession between the priest and the sinner.

Afterwards, Father Solon rebuked a naïve reporter who had pressed him about what the two of them had talked about that morning. "I will have nothing further to say in the matter," the priest told him. "My answer is final."

When asked if he had any last words, Hart said that he had nothing to say.

72

At 11am, the jailhouse door opened and the procession to the gallows began. Sheriff Burbank led the way, closely followed by Father Solon, and Father Lamb of Belvidere. Behind the two priests came John Hart, his hands tied behind his back, escorted by two sheriff's deputies. They ascended the scaffold. When Hart got to the trap door, Burbank asked him if he wanted to sit in the chair provided.

Hart preferred to stand.

Burbank began the grim task of preparing Hart to hang, binding his arms, legs, ankles, and then, finally, affixing the noose firmly around his neck.

"Do you have any last words, John?" the Sheriff asked.

"Upon the advice of my spiritual advisor, I have nothing to say," Hart responded.

And with that, Father Solon stepped up to him with a crucifix. Hart kissed it. Then, as is customary, Hart's body was covered in a loose white shroud, and a cap was placed over his head. From this moment forward, there would be nothing but darkness for Hart.

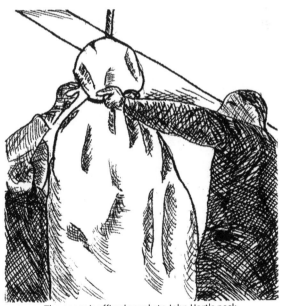

The noose is affixed snugly to John Hart's neck.
As is customary, the condemned wears a shroud and a hood.

Behind a nearby partition, an anonymous individual peered through a peephole, waiting for a special signal from the Sheriff to release the trapdoor.

At 11:04 Sheriff Burbank gave the signal. The trap door sprung open with a loud crashing sound. John Hart's body plunged downward, the rope gave a sharp jerk, and his neck snapped instantly. According to witnesses, Hart's body convulsed once, then hung limp. In spite of a broken neck, Hart still had a faint heartbeat. As such, every five minutes, a doctor came forward to check his pulse as it grew weaker. After fifteen minutes, John Hart was declared officially dead. For the most part, this had been a 'clean' hanging, save for a rope cut above Hart's throat which bled profusely. With little fanfare, John Hart's body was cut down and released to the local undertaker.

That evening, less than six hours after John Hart's execution, Fathers Solon and Lamb officiated over a brief private funeral service for him. The only people who attended Hart's funeral and burial were two of his brothers, his Uncle Con, and several cousins. John Hart's mother, Bridget Hart, declined to attend. It was most likely that she chose to grieve privately, as she had been doing for some time. Certainly the events of that day - both an execution and a funeral - would have been too much stress for a mother to handle.

John Hart Jr. Guilty of murdering his two sisters.
The second person to be executed in Winnebago County.

Very few people took particular notice as Hart's plain black casket was transported up North Main Street to St. Mary's Cemetery. He would be buried in a family plot, alongside his sisters, Mary and Nellie. But unlike his sisters, John Hart's grave would be unmarked. That night, with each shovel of fresh dirt tossed on his grave, a very dark chapter in their family history was officially closed.

It is highly unlikely that any jury would have acquitted John Hart by reason of insanity. Just as John Hart felt no remorse for his two sisters whom he killed, the citizens of Rockford had no remorse for him as he dangled from the gallows. On the day after Hart's execution, the local newspaper published the following poem, written by a local citizen:

'The Murdered Sisters'

God above have mercy on them,
They are in their lonely grave,
Murdered by their heartless brother
No one near their life to save.
The very one who should protect them,
Help them through a world of strife,
Was the one that stole behind them
Took away their precious life.
All young men pray, take warning,
Of John Hart, his dreadful fate,
Let his sad end be a lesson,
But for him it is too late

By Rosy Pollard
(Rockford Daily Register Gazette, March 17, 1894)

The trauma and heartache that Bridget Hart and her family experienced between 1892 and March of 1894 is almost unthinkable. Mrs. Hart's faith undoubtedly played a large role in helping her to cope and endure. One is reminded of the popular Catholic image of Our Lady of Sorrows, its depiction of the Holy Mother with seven daggers in her heart.

In a similar sense, Bridget Hart carried four daggers. Her suffering and loss is hard for most people to fathom. And it is harder yet to imagine the mercy and forgiveness that she displayed toward her son. Instead of disowning him, as many mothers would, Mrs. Hart defended John Hart and his character to the very end, in spite of overwhelming evidence which suggested that she ought to do otherwise.

In 1897, Bridget Hart sold the farm and quietly moved into the city of Rockford, where she spent the remainder of her years. When Mrs. Hart died on October 30, 1918, at the age of eighty, she was remembered as:

"...a woman of splendid nobility of character, whose desire was to be of service to those with whom she associated."
(Rockford Republic, October 18, 1918)

Author's Notes:
I researched the basic facts of the case using old newspaper back issues.
My account of the actual murders is a dramatization, a purely speculative version of how the attacks *may* have occurred. Because John Hart never actually confessed to the murders, we cannot be certain as to the specific details (i.e. - the manner in which he attacked the girls or in what order he attacked them). Crime scene investigations in the 1890's were very limited, ranging somewhere between crude and non-existent. The best, and only known, first-hand account that we have is Nellie's deathbed statement. Also, based on the physical evidence, Mary put up a great struggle.

SOURCES:
Chicago Daily Inter Ocean
Rockford Daily Register Gazette
Rockford Morning Star
Rockford Republic
History of the Winnebago County Sheriff's Office

NEED FOR ANOTHER

ANOTHER

TERRY STOLZ

A single soul in a vessel of love
A heart that burns with the salient quality of Armageddon...
A heart that runs cold like a winter night...
on the front-lines of The Western Front

Feast one's eyes on the heaviness of heart
and the radiant colors of the South of France
Searching far and wide for the warmth of a sentient being
The quest for eternal bliss
The discovery of another life

The cries of mating fill the silence of the night
No longer are you one, nor, are you two...
You are the hope...of more to come!

THE END OF DESTINY

KARNA TECLA

Madam Alexander turned the well-manicured hand over. "This is your dominant hand, is it not?" The medium pierced Elizabeth's eyes, causing a cold shiver to race down Elizabeth's spine.

"Yes." Elizabeth's voice sounded like someone had placed a mute on her vocal cords.

"And you want to know about your past, but not your present? Or future? Unusual. Most want to know what lies ahead of them in life."

"What I truly need to know is the *why* of where I am today."

♦　　♦　　♦　　♦　　♦

Two months ago, Elizabeth had begun having wild, lucid dreams. When she had shared the first one with Vicky, her best friend, Vicky had laughed.

"You've got to stop reading those classics before you go to bed," Vicky had chided.

That was the one and only dream that Elizabeth had shared, but there had been others; others that had built upon that first dream. In the second, the colors of everyone's clothes had begun to fade and the style was more roaring 20's. In the next, everyone's bodies were wasting away.

That weekend, Elizabeth scoured the library for volumes on dream interpretation. "Damn this Bible belt community and their lack of open-mindedness!"

In the end, Elizabeth had driven to the city, hoping that the book store there could be of better service.

Elizabeth scanned the store: first for people who she might know, or who might know her, and second for someone who wouldn't be alarmed by her request. Her search landed upon a young clerk in the middle of the store.

"Excuse me," Elizabeth prompted.

"Hi! My name is Christine. How may I help you today?"

"Do you have a section on dreams? Or books on dream interpretation?"

A twinkle in Christine's eyes reached out over her black eye liner and shadow. "Right this way."

Christine lead the way to the back of the store, and over to a semi-discreet corner. "We don't get many requests for these, but I also don't know why they keep them buried back here. Let me know if you need anything more."

Elizabeth pulled down the volume that declared itself to be a 'dream dictionary'. Thumbing through the entries, she found what she was seeking:

coffin: symbolizes the womb; feeling confined, restricted, and lacking personal freedom.

Elizabeth slammed the book shut.

That night, stick figures rose from the coffin in her dream. Each had a number on card that hung around their inconsequential necks. In the background, a voice rose to crescendo.

♦   ♦   ♦   ♦   ♦

Madam Alexander dragged a finger along one of the lines in Elizabeth's palm, bringing Elizabeth's focus back to the little room surrounding her, and the medium holding her hand.

"This is your heart line. This, your head line. And this your life line," Madam Alexander said, tracing each as she spoke. "Your heart line tells me that you are a one man woman who is content in her current relationship." Madam Alexander looked into Elizabeth's eyes. "You have a wonderful husband, don't you?"

Elizabeth nodded.

"Your head line tells me that you are very adventurous and enthusiastic. That is, until recently. Because something is causing you to be uncomfortable."

Elizabeth's eyes widened. It was as if this woman was reading a book that had been written about Elizabeth herself.

"Your life line tells me that you are healthy and energetic." Madam Alexander took Elizabeth's other hand. "But I also know that you are an old, old soul." After a pause, the medium stared once more into Elizabeth's eyes. "Tell me about your dream last night."

"My. . .but how did you know?"

"Shhh," the medium soothed. "Now tell me. Were there a large number of non-descript people standing around in a non-descript room?"

Elizabeth nodded.

"Your dream in an explanation of what you know in your heart. The fact that you have been trying to figure everything out is a sign of your soul's true age. Do you know your number?"

Elizabeth closed her eyes. In her mind she was staring at her stick figure reflection – the number on her card bold, and clearly printed. It read:

346 – 3 – 4 – Z

"The first number, 346, represents the number of times you have reincarnated. The second number, 3, represents the continent to which you have been assigned. The 4 represents the living standards you have continually been born into. And the Z informs the authorities that this will be the last reincarnation for you."

"What happens then?"

"Then, my dear, you will become part of the Earth, to help nourish those who come after you."

SKATE NIGHT

JENNY MATHEWS

School skate night is as close to a grade school disco as it gets. A
gangly seven year old clip-clops across the floor with her arms doing
a wild and jerky air-swim, next to another's dance moves in which
she leans way down low, bending at the waist, doing a circle motion
with her arms in perfect 'rolling down the river' precision. Lip gloss
and fingerless gloves cease to be dress up items and become totally
serious accessories to eye rolling aloofness. Sitting on a wall is an art
form in cool, not something Humpty Dumpty did. Parents are
invisible as little brothers strive to become feral children under the
benches, where the carpet glows bright and *Cheetos* are hitting the
floor. For two glorious hours the world spins and rolls in screams of
joy and shared nachos.

WRAPPED IN IVY

KATHI KRESOL

"If she had looked into his eyes at that very moment she would have seen the inferno that she had thrown him into."
- Llàrime, *'Craving U'*

Anyone who knew the little family before that July day would say that one thing was certain: Vernon Plager loved his wife and daughter more than anything. His marriage was good. They had had a rough patch the year before, but now he and his wife, Ivy, were getting along really well. Vernon, who was 28, blamed most of their problems on the fact that Ivy, 22 in 1928, was so young when they fell in love. She was only sixteen when they were married and then the baby, Lois, came. Ivy had gotten restless. She struggled with all of the responsibility of being a young mother and wife.

Paul Reed, 22, had entered the picture in 1927. That was when everything had turned bad in their marriage. Paul lived across the street from Ivy and Vernon. He had seen her in the neighborhood and found her attractive. Ivy was small, fair skinned, and was said to have had 'vivid blue eyes'.

The pair met on July 4, when Paul and Ivy were outside on the sidewalk lighting firecrackers. Reed got Ivy's phone number and called her repeatedly through July and August. Paul was finally able to convince Ivy to go riding with him while her husband was at work. Ivy went for a drive with Reed and became smitten with the young man. Paul never had a girl before, and Ivy was bored with her life. Paul made her laugh. The rides led to more, and then they eventually spent a night in a local hotel, named The Chick House.

Next they left on a train for Peoria, and then for Davenport, for two weeks in October of 1927. The papers would later call it an 'elopement'.

Vernon's brother, Floyd, had married Ivy's sister. Floyd came and got him one awful night when Ivy had returned to Rockford. They went to the police and followed them to Floyd's house. Ivy was there with Reed, in what would be considered a 'compromising position'.

Later, when asked what the couple were wearing, the police officer who had been on the scene replied, "They were in bed."

Ivy and Reed were arrested on charges of disruption of the peace and taken to jail. Vernon let Ivy spend the night there, but went to talk to her the next morning. He offered to let her come home. He would forgive her everything, as long as she came home to him and their little daughter.

Ivy did return home, and they worked on their marriage. Vernon even agreed to give up smoking his pipe - something he knew that she detested. They were working as a team to repair their marriage and build a good life together. He bought her new furniture and surprised her with little bouquets of roses, her favorite flower. Vernon also bought her a very pretty ring for her birthday. Ivy told people that Vernon was good to her. He made sure they had a comfortable home, and that she and little Lois were very happy.

They had moved into a new upper apartment on Howard Avenue in the beginning of July. Paul Reed did not just go away though. They would see him pass by the new house and sometimes, when they were out with their daughter, they would notice Paul there in the background, watching them.

On Wednesday, July 18, 1928, the family went for a drive to Byron. There was an outdoor concert that Vernon knew Ivy would love. He came home from work and they drove there and listened to the music before heading back home. Vernon thought he saw Paul Reed's car going south on Route 2 when they were headed north. It worried him because he knew that Paul Reed had stopped by the house that morning to see Ivy. Reed still loved Ivy and wanted to know if she would run away with him again. Vernon trusted Ivy when she said that she had told Reed that she was staying with her husband and her little girl.

They followed their usual bedtime ritual that night and he knelt down by Lois' bedside to say prayers with her. Later, Ivy stated that they heard noises out in the alley but they didn't think too much about it. Vernon hadn't even gone to check on it.

The next morning was a work day for Vernon. He kissed Lois and Ivy goodbye and walked around to the back of the home where he parked his car, an old two door that was owned by the Crosley Radio Company (where he worked for his brother, C.A. Plager).

The quiet, summer morning was ripped apart by a loud explosion just before 9am. Ivy looked out and saw Vernon's car blown to pieces. Witnesses would later say that they saw Vernon attempt to start his car and that it would not start. He went back into the house for a moment and came back outside. He crawled into the car and stepped on the starter button. Vernon's body was lifted twenty feet in the air from the blast, "higher than the wires" according to one man, and then his body plunged back into the wreckage of what had once been his car. His hip area was obviously crushed, while his left leg was twisted around his neck. His intestines were on the pavement next to him. For a brief while he was unconscious, but regained consciousness quickly.

Vernon came to, lying in the street, amongst the detritus that had once been his automobile. Ivy rushed to his side and grabbed his hand. She stood up with a suddenness, saying, "Oh, I can't even look at you!" and ran back into the house, grabbing their little daughter on the way in.

Lois, their daughter, wanted to go and see her daddy. So much so that she was hysterically screaming for Ivy to let her go. Two policemen showed up, lifted Vernon's horribly mangled body into the police ambulance. He was in a phenomenal amount of excruciating pain. So much so that Vernon had begged the policeman to shoot him. He also told the police that they should find Paul Reed to question him about the explosion.

They rushed Vernon to the hospital, but there was nothing that the doctors there could do for him. In the end, they simply attempted to alleviate his overwhelming pain. Vernon died, shortly after arrival, in the operating room.

Vernon's car after the explosion.
From the July 19, 1928 Rockford Daily Register.
(Used with permission from The Rockford Register Star & rrstar.com)

Vernon's funeral was held at the Fred Olson Undertaking Parlor. There were at least five-hundred "morbid" people wandering around outside, attempting to see the pretty "girl-widow" as Ivy was called in the paper. Ivy was accompanied to the funeral home by Police Matron, Ida Patterson, since she was in police custody at the time. She cried during the ceremony, especially when the pastor said, "Death was on the track of Mr. Plager." Ivy stepped up to the coffin to look at her husband's face once last time. Everyone mentioned how handsome he looked, even in death. The coffin hid the damage caused by the blast. A relative held little Lois up so that she, too, could see her father. Then the family watched as the lid closed on Vernon for the last time.

When Ivy left the building, photographers actually jumped on taxis and other cars to get a good angle for a picture. Vernon's body was sent to Pearl City, where most of his family lived, for burial. Ivy was allowed to go to the funeral in Pearl City (once more with Police Matron, Ida Patterson). Lois, the Plager's five year old daughter, rode with her mother and the police woman to Pearl City. There were over five hundred attendees at Vernon's funeral.

Paul Reed had been very busy all week prior to the bombing. He went to a store in Rockford to inquire about purchasing dynamite to blow up a spring on his camping spot in Wisconsin. They refused to sell it to him. Reed picked up his twenty-two-year-old nephew, Kenneth Reed, and they drove down to Dixon, where Kenneth's father, Arthur, lived. Arthur was Paul's forty-five-year-old brother. Paul told Arthur that he needed to buy some dynamite for the spring. Arthur had to ride over to a neighbor's, Shelby Riddle's, farm to give a bid for a job that Riddle needed done on the farm and Arthur was meeting him. While he was there, Arthur asked Riddle where to purchase dynamite, mentioning to him that his nephew, Paul, needed to blow up a spring.

Riddle told him that the only person that had any dynamite would be Ben Good, the Highway Commissioner. He kept the dynamite in a shed at the quarry near Polo. The men all headed back to Arthur's place for a late supper. After supper, Paul asked Arthur for a crowbar and he and Kenneth left in Reed's car.

They drove over to the quarry, according to Kenneth's later statement. They parked up on the road and walked down to the shed. There was a lock on the door, so Paul used a ledge to gain access to the roof. From there, he lifted some roof planks off with the crowbar. Then he dropped down inside the shed, leaving Kenneth outside as a lookout.

Paul was inside for about ten minutes before he crawled back out on the roof. There, he used the crowbar to hammer the planks back in place. It was dark. And perhaps it was due to this all-consuming darkness that he failed to notice that he had left an open spot. This point would become evidence, and would be used against him later. When Paul dropped back down to the ground, Kenneth could see a coil of wire and three sticks of dynamite in Paul's pants.

Police arrested Paul Reed when he surrendered to the Ogle County Police within hours of the murder. They arrested Ivy Plager as well, on the suspicion that she was an accessory to the murder of her husband, but she was released after several days in custody. She went to stay with her sister, and her husband's brother, Floyd, on Greenwood Avenue while awaiting Reed's trial.

After the bombing, on the morning of July 19, 1928, Paul Reed's car was found in Mount Morris, Illinois by Detectives Strote and Williams. They found a small coil of wire when they searched the car. They recognized it as being of the same sort as the wire that was found twisted on the starter wire of Vernon's car.

Paul was arraigned whereupon he engaged the services of Dixon, Bracken, Devine, and Dixon, a local law firm. They selected Attorney Charles H. Linscott to represent Reed in the proceedings.

At the Coroner's Inquest, in the undertaking rooms, Fred Olson asked Ivy Plager if she cared for Paul Reed. She said that she had loved Paul Reed once, but not any longer. Paul Reed was also questioned during the inquest but, on the advice of his attorney, refused to testify. During this time, he was described as a gaunt, hollow eyed, young man.

Ivy's father came to visit her during her time in jail. He was a stern, hard old man who didn't offer any comfort or succor to his daughter. "What are you going to do when this is all over?" her father asked, without so much as a greeting.

Ivy wasn't sure, but stated that she was thinking of coming home. This statement was met by silence from her father. When Police Matron Ida Patterson mentioned to Ivy's father that Ivy needed a little money to help her buy a new pair of shoes, he stood up and walked away without saying another word.

Ivy Plager in jail after the murder of her husband.
From the July 19, 1928 Rockford Daily Register.
(Used with permission from The Rockford Register Star & rrstar.com)

Police searched the rooming house where Paul Reed was staying, but it was two newsmen that made the most dramatic discovery. They found sticks of dynamite and nitroglycerin fuses wrapped in old newspaper in a hole under the basement stairs. Chicago Tribune reporter Robert W. Wood, and Chicago Journal reporter Michael Fielding, found the incriminating evidence on July 23. They approached the Landlady of the rooming house, Mrs. Lena Hawkins, and explained they were 'special investigators'. It was this act of duplicity which convinced Mrs. Hawkins to grant them access to the house and Reed's rooms. They started in the attic and made their way down to the basement where there was storage space for items belonging to the roomers.

Police had already searched the house, including the basement - twice - but missed the hole that was discovered under the stairway, toward the last stair tread. Wood and Fielding called the State's Attorney, William Knight, and he came to the house. They extracted the packages holding the dynamite and fuses from under the stairway with Knight as a witness.

The men took the packages to the living room, where Mrs. Hawkinson joined them. They were unsettled to see that the "small glycerin fuse, contained in a bright copper shell, was waxed onto the shell", setting it in place. The three men felt that this must have been prepared in the basement, since doing so made the dynamite far more dangerous to move thereafter. Mrs. Hawkinson was much more concerned about whether she would have to testify than the fact there was a dangerous explosive located in her house.

Paul Reed was charged with First Degree Murder with the option of the Death Penalty. Reed's was the first trial in Winnebago County where, if found guilty, execution would be carried out by electric chair. Winnebago County had four previous cases that had resulted in the death penalty, but the guilty men had all been hanged.

Reed's trial began on December 3, 1928. His defense counsel was C.H. Linscott, who was assisted by Jerome Dixon. The prosecutor was William D. Knight. The judge presiding over the case was Circuit Judge Arthur A. Fisher. The defense won a major point at the outset of the trial when Vernon's dying words that Paul Reed had set the dynamite that exploded was not permitted to be admitted as evidence.

At the trial, every seat was taken. The courtroom would normally seat around 350 people but each day the spectators would smash together until the attendant crowd reached closer to 500. Some of the more creative women would bring their sack lunches and eat right in their seats so that they didn't lose them during recess.

Both Arthur Reed, the defendant's brother, and Kenneth Reed, the defendant's nephew, testified for the state. Arthur explained that Paul told him that he was going on his annual camping trip, and that he needed the dynamite to deal with an offending spring that ran through his camp site. Kenneth recounted the story of their having stolen the dynamite from the quarry shed.

Another witness who caused quite a stir on the stand was Edward Rydberg. Rydberg carried with him a little tin box that he bumped against several items of furniture on his way to the stand. Then he announced that he worked on the road construction crew and was the expert on handling explosives. He opened the little tin box, and nonchalantly removed two sticks of dynamite from within. Then he proceeded to plunk them down on the judge's bench. This action caused some nervous laughter from the courtroom and understandably, the judge. Rydberg seemed to enjoy his effect on the crowd and a perpetual grin remained upon his face as he testified.

Paul Reed, convicted murderer of Vern Plager.
From the July 24, 1928 Morning Star
(Used with permission from The Rockford Register Star & rrstar.com)

The defense counsel's questions of Rydberg, and of Motorcycle Policeman Stewart Mulford, led spectators to suspect that the defense was attempting to prove that the explosion was caused by a faulty gas tank rather than dynamite. The counsel hammered away at the witnesses, attempting to lay the groundwork for reasonable doubt.

Everyone wanted to see the 'star' of the case, Iva Plager (or Ivy, as she was best known). They wanted to see the young lady who one man was willing to kill another for. She was described in the papers and "mysterious and elusive".

The testimony of Police Detective Tony Shakotzus was by far the most dramatic in the trial up to that point. He told the story of finding Ivy and Paul Reed together in Floyd Plager's home on Greenwood Avenue (Floyd was Vernon's brother, and his wife was

Ivy's sister). The couple were found together on the morning of November 5, 1927, after they had returned from Iowa. The room was silent as Shakotzus gave his testimony. The several hundred people in the room seemed to lean forward to hear the story. These were the first public details of the intimate relationship between Ivy and the man on trial for the murder of her husband. The crowd exploded with comments after the testimony. The judge banged his gavel to restore order, and threatened to clear the room to get them to quiet back down.

Ivy finally testified on December 6 to a packed courtroom. Ivy answered as State's Attorney William Knight hurled question after question at her. She hesitated on describing her husband's death scene and a sob escaped her. Though she tried to avoid answering, Ivy was given no choice. She sobbed as she described the way she found her husband. "He was lying in the alley, his legs were off, as near as I can remember, his body was out, his stomach was out and lying beside him. Oh, dear, it was terrible."

Ivy endured a grueling 110 minutes of badgering by the State's Attorney and the Defense Attorney. She told of meeting Paul Reed on July 4, 1927. The Defense Counsel Linscott tried to show that it was Ivy that pursued Reed for the illicit meetings.

Ivy also told of the day before the bombing. Paul Reed stopped at her house. She testified that he was angry. So angry, in fact, that he was shaking. He kissed her and asked her if he had any chance at all with her. Ivy told him that he shouldn't come back ever again. Reed told her, "You are going to wait too long. Something is going to happen."

Paul Reed testified in his defense on December 6. His testimony started with his personal history. He was born in Rockford but moved to Palisades, Colorado. While he was there he worked in a coal mine, on a cattle ranch, and on an oil field. It was while he worked in the oil field that he learned to handle dynamite. He came back to Rockford and got a job at the National Lock Company and, most recently, he was employed as a draftsman at the Ingersoll Milling Machine Company.

After the jury deliberated, Paul Reed was convicted of the murder of Vernon Plager, and sentenced to life in prison in Joliet. He left Rockford as a 23-year-old young man. When he arrived in Joliet, he became Prisoner number 2503. He was transferred to Pontiac

Reformatory in 1940, suffering from tuberculosis. He later died there of the disease in 1947.

He denied the killing of Vernon Plager until the day that he died.

Vernon's family was very hurt by some of the things reported in the newspaper. Some articles reported that Vernon had 'stepped out' with other girls, that Vernon's family were keeping Ivy's daughter, Lois, from her, and that Vernon had left the family penniless. These reports supposedly came from the Defense Council, likely because they were trying to discredit Vernon. It's curious to consider that anyone could seek justification for blowing a man apart in front of his family.

C.A. Plager spoke for the Plager family. They had taken Lois, the 5-year-old daughter, to Pearl City to stay with Vernon's mother only while Ivy was incarcerated. C.A. also explained that his brother never had gone out with another woman, nor would he. Vernon worked as a brakeman at Central Amusement Park. As such, it was his job to ride with young ladies (or young men) that were by themselves. It short, it was a required facet of his job to accompany single riders. C.A. spoke of his brother as a hard worker that was willing to forgive his wife in order to keep his little family together. Vernon had once told his brother that he loved Ivy so much he couldn't live without her. Vernon's actions after Ivy's indiscretion only served to bolster these claims.

The romance that started one hot July day with fireworks ended on another day in July with dynamite. It was all so tragic, and completely pointless. Vernon was dead at 28 years old. Paul Reed never left prison, his life was, essentially, over at the tender age of 22. Little Lois Plager had to grow up without her loving father. Ivy moved to Chicago for a while, only to return to Rockford. She was employed as a maid for a family on Harlem Boulevard. Ivy eventually married again, and lived to be ninety-seven years old.

Hopefully, she and Lois got their happy ending.

Sources:

"Ivy Plager Sees Husband Buried; Returns to Jail." 21 July 1928 *Rockford Daily Republic* (Rockford, IL): 1

"Ivy Echoes Dead Husband's Words: Reed did it." 21 July 1928 *Rockford Daily Republic* (Rockford, IL): 1

"I'll Get Him", Wife Told Mate." 21 July 1928 *Rockford Daily Republic* (Rockford, IL): 1

"He Was Always Good to Me." 22 July 1928 *Rockford Morning Star* (Rockford, IL): 1

"Nephew Says Suspect Stole High Explosives." 21 July 1928 *Rockford Morning Star* (Rockford, IL): 1

"Two Sticks, Fuses, and Nitroglycerin Found Under Stairs." 24 July 1928 *Rockford Morning Star* (Rockford, IL):1

"Ivy can Claim her Child." 26 July 1928 *Rockford Daily Republic* (Rockford, IL): 18

"Contend Plager was Not Killed by Bomb Made of Dynamite." 5 December 1928 *Rockford Morning Star* (Rockford, IL): 1

"Narrative of Arrest is Told by Detectives." 6 December 1928 *Daily Register Gazette* (Rockford, IL): 1

"Court Fans Bring Lunch to Reed Trial." 6 December 1928 *Daily Register Gazette* (Rockford, IL): 1

"Court Fans Perk Up as Iva Testifies." 7 December 1928 *Rockford Morning Star* (Rockford, IL): 1

"Sobs while Telling of Finding Husband While Dying After Blast." 7 December 1928 *Rockford Morning Star* (Rockford, IL): 1

"Firecrackers Blossomed in Love Affair." 8 December 1928 *Rockford Daily Republic* (Rockford, IL): 2

"Prison Grim Climax to Love Crime." 19 December 1928 *Rockford Daily Republic* (Rockford, IL): 1

"City's Last Bombing Hit Its Target." 24 June 1957 *Rockford Register- Republic* (Rockford, IL):

WARMTH

CASANDRA GOLDSMITH

106

Clouds begin to form, as night draws to a close
Their bodies wrestle against one another
to create shape
The cool, crisp air stings my mouth
I am feeling pure calm for the first time
Nothing in the world
Can disturb this peace
Chills form on my skin
Knowledge of this pending fury
Thunder strikes!
I am cold
Night returns with force
I smile
I am not afraid
My arms wrap about my chest
I feel warmth
The storm descends.

THE BATTERY MAN

HEATH D. ALBERTS

I awaken with a jolt. My receptors initialize, and I perceive an external source of light. It is the sun. Or at least, it is what is visible of it through the haze. The haze is not further quantifiable, so I cannot describe it beyond 'haze'. All around me lay ruination; destruction; catastrophe; <Synonym #7293 Not Found>; blight. Nothing living stirs for as far as I am able to perceive. And my perception is quite acute.

My servos warm, and within infinitesimally minute fractions of an adannu, I am once more capable of ambulation. Battery power registers at 85%. If I am conservative, this will be enough for 47 adannus. If I am not, I could utilize it all before the next three sunrises.

I attempt to acclimate, so as to discern my 'where', but triangulation is proving impossible. Satellites #37, #106, & #55 should be at appropriate apogee to permit them to assist, yet I find that communication with any of them will not occur with success. I attempt a moon bounce off of other satellites, but not even the moon beam returns. Most likely this is due to my calculations being incorrect as to its whereabouts, or the atmospheric contamination currently present. This is most troublesome.

My internal clock tells me that it is 00:03, Sphere Time. This is countermanded by the presence of the sun. I therefore discern that my on-board computer battery is defunct, and will require replacement. I similarly acknowledge the date, and then discard it as being false as well. This confirms my suspicions about my calculations: without correct time and date data, I cannot work out the spatial whereabouts of the moon.

As I ascertain my personal space, I find a portion of a wall, a roughly three-foot high by eight-foot long corner that is familiar to me. It is part of laboratory forty-two. The rest of the lab - or where it should be - is gone. I surmise that the devastation and rubble around me comprises some or all of the remainder of it. I confirm this by visually locating compositional bits of my fallen brethren. I scan for a torso, but find none intact within visual ranging. I will attempt to keep this action of battery replacement as a priority, though it will only allow me to superficially discern date and time from the moment of installation and setting forward.

Effecting an upright position, my radiation monitor screams to life. It registers 1408.3 hilams. My scientific lexicon enacts itself, essentially unbidden. This is more than 122 times the lethal dose for a human being. Therefore, I surmise logically that there should be no living humans in the vicinity. Utterly alone, I consider my options. In the end, I choose a path of localized scouting.

Moving in a sequential grid, it takes me more than two-point-three adannus to successfully traverse a one square gisisu area. My findings are thus: all structures within the immediate vicinity, as well as vicinities visible outside of the grid area, are destroyed. Most entirely, but some remnants remain which allow me to quantify my relational location. Everyone is indeed dead, or absent from proximity. I surmise that no life forms within a great distance are animate. This is presumed to be the result of a weapon which cleaves atoms. A large one.

By developing a rudimentary grid of the buildings thus far identified and located, I am able to overlay this data onto my existing map of the complex, and the city without. From this I may then extrapolate direction. In doing so, I will allow my binnacle to be digitally set for future use, when familiar landmarks no longer present themselves. I am endowed with a map of the continent itself, though it is only rudimentary outside of the confines of known habitation(s). It could be more detailed, but I was not provided one as such. This may prove troublesome.

Logic circuits begin estimating the cumulative probability of what my next task should entail. The result takes .0000000132 adannus to arrive. Battery power is now at 84%. There are no functioning charging stations within the vicinity, nor are there any salvageable batteries to be had from my defunct brethren. I must go abroad and seek out a new means of charging/recharging. A photovoltaic attachment would be ideal, but they were uncommon in this area. What my map defines as 'Sub-Station 27', far to the north of my location, is where they were predominantly used, and even then only on the field defense units. This, my logic unit suggests, should be my goal. It is a trip of more than 37 gasisus. Over flat terrain, this would utilize 94% battery charge; over rugged terrain, more. Thus, I am forced to concede that success is only possible if some sort of charging method - or external power source - may be found, as I would be left with a negative power surplus.

Before moving forward with my journey, I self-lube. I find that servo #34 - left knee, camber right - is not functioning properly. I take it offline, so that it will 'float' under the influence of the surrounding servos. I will have to use all due caution on rugged terrain, so as not to overcompensate, and thereby lose gyroscopic center mass. There is also a marginal leak in servo #129 - left shoulder rotator, rear. This servo I leave on-line, but I shunt the lube from returning further to it to conserve as much as possible. I cannot estimate when more lube will be available to me. I also re-route my basic programming to work around the use of motions that require this servo joint, to allow it to do so without first requesting an 'override further' clearance. This way, no lasting damage is done.

Finally, I switch my cooling fan units to tube mode. This will draw air through my superstructure in five distinct areas, but will use heat sinks in those areas to dissipate heat, rather than allowing fan-forced air flow through my superstructure. This will cause more heat to build up, but I deem it an acceptable risk in order to prevent debris from entering my superstructure. The air is fouled here, and does not seem to change as the winds periodically sweep over me from the north.

Ambulation proves to be fairly uneventful. Having never done it over this sort of terrain before, or over a distance this great, my logic unit offered a marginal concern for my ability to achieve success. This seems unfounded now. And future calculations will be modified to include the new data which I am gleaning as I ambulate further.

◆   ◆   ◆   ◆   ◆

No relevant data has occurred for 1.2 adannus. I have traversed a marginal incline which I have identified as 'Zaqru Rise'. I began to detect ejecta, and land-flotsam, some .7 adannus past, but felt it insignificant to me without accompanying data. I crest the hill, and on the leeward side should be found the residential population center 'Baltu'. In its place, I encounter only further, and more substantial, wreckage - both physical and remnant human. My radiation monitor registers a reading of 1734.3 hilams. This would concur with the level of burning and bone crystallization which is evident in the partial, human skeletal remains that survived the blast, while still being identifiable as such. Skulls and femurs are the most prolific, salted with an occasional, random bone, and many 'hand and digits' combinations - sans some or all of them.

As I move closer to the former location of the center of the town,

I find a sizeable crater. This is most likely the ground-zero point of the weapon used to enact the damage in evidence all around me. I surmise a class-II weapon. This is in congruency with my findings at the laboratory as well. A class-I would have cratered the entire hill. Here, bedrock is evident in places, but the hill structure remains in-tact.

Ambulating through the town, I begin to <no word for frame of reference> what occurred. What caused this devastation to be brought upon the residents here; the scientists and scholars back at the lab? Was it an accidental detonation of stored devices? If so, why were the devices necessary in these locales? As soon as this specific line of inquiry passes through my processor cluster my Social Archive makes itself known. I did not know that I was imbued with such. It loads, and I find a secondary sub-routine being launched as well: 'Expanded Dictionary'. It dovetails in with my 'Expanded Thesaurus', which I now realize was loaded on boot up. The loading of the Thesaurus, but not the Dictionary, is counter-intuitive. I posit that this anomalous load must have occurred due to some as yet unknown, further damage within my internal electronics.

'Ponder' comes to the fore, as the dictionary scans my audit trail for anomalies. I begin to ponder what may have occurred to everything around me.

The Social Archive settles on entry #1,324,161: WAR: 'A state of armed conflict between different factions or differing groups within a quantifiable area.'

'War' is what happened here. 'War' is what obliterated all of these lives; all of these things around me.

Utility software embedded within my sub-processors indicates that my memory and software-utilization functions may be damaged or functioning improperly. This is in agreement with my personal observations as well. The utility software itemizes a boot log, and within it I see numerous other sub-routine, archival, and specialty software that failed to load at the moment of initial reboot. I am asked whether I wish them to be loaded now, and I elect to do so. Within moments, a flood of new and useful data becomes available to me, and perspective and clarity are achieved more precisely.

The husk of the town I am now leaving in my virtual wake was indeed known as 'Baltu', and was a part of the nation-state of

Abanyarahhu.

Abanyarahhu was comprised of 135 population centers, 17 military installations, and *<no quantity registered>* supporting commercial and industrial complexes found scattered throughout.

To the west lay the nation of Aksu. Aksu was found on this continent, and was comprised of 96 population centers, 13 military installations, and *<no quantity registered>* supporting commercial and industrial complexes found scattered throughout.

No other nations, principalities, factions, states, or social entities existed upon this continent. This leads me to believe that either war is indeed the correct interpretation, or something called 'internal conflict' may have occurred. This second choice makes little sense, as it would only weaken one of two evenly matched factions. I therefore hypothesize that war is the correct notion.

Already I am finding my vocabulary bolstered. This prompts a memory within me. I analyze the origins of the memory, and find a cache of several others - seven to be exact. These memories are video logs totaling .1 adannus in length, cumulatively. I examine each as my ambulation continues, and the worthless remains of *Baltu* recede into the distance.

Memories 1-6 are all short, and relatively similar in composition. They consist of a boot up phase, a self-diagnostic, and then audio and video of a human called Ana Dabdu, and his assistant, Ana Rebu. They speak to one another, in a manner commensurate with their superior-inferior roles, about the results that I myself am reviewing with them. Nothing of immediate use can be gleaned from this, so I move on.

Memory seven is altogether different, and consists of the majority of the space occupied. Memory seven begins with a panic-stricken Ana Rebu shouting to someone I cannot see. No response is recorded, and then a thunderous explosion rocks the entire building. My sensors indicate that the explosion was massive, but far enough away to be insubstantial to our well-being at that present moment. Moments later, a shockwave is felt, and Ana Rebu's hands and jaw go slack. Just after this, he does something within my torso cavity that I cannot identify.

"Dear Alu, no!" he beseeches the workspace around him. I recognize this as an attempt at interaction with a deity. No recorded response occurs from said deity. He then crumples into his stool, and sits slumped before me for several moments, looking at the floor, and otherwise remaining stoic and inanimate. Several more moments pass, and he once more springs into action. With a feverish purpose, I watch as he looks for something. After opening seven tray drawers in a nearby work counter, he finds what he is seeking, and once more addresses me.

"This," he says, "Is history. *Our* history: The history of the Abanyarahhu and Aksu peoples. If you survive this, make sure that future generations learn from it. It is vastly important. Do you understand?"

Here, the audit trail underlying the recorded memory indicates that I responded in the affirmative. He resumes his place upon the stool, his hand moves toward my data slot compartment, and this is when the walls around us explode. They reveal a blinding flash beyond where they - only moments before - stood silent vigil. In the fraction of an adannu, I witness his discorporation and vaporization, before I am thrown backward and into a mechanic's pit. This explains how I survived the blast and fallout, but not how I found myself out of the pit upon rebooting. Probability dictates that this one niggling fact will forever remain a mystery.

Here, the audio/visual portion of the memory ends. The remainder of the memory is just the audit trail assessing and documenting the damage (here the servo and lube issue are both recorded), and documenting the emergency shutdown. This is all.

More than anything, this gives even further positive reinforcement to my supposition that war was the catalyst behind the destruction that I have thus far witnessed.

◆   ◆   ◆   ◆   ◆

As I cross an open meadow, I begin to reassess some of my observations. The meadow before me is lush, and the town behind me was heavily overgrown. With all mental units now on-line and functioning, I come to the realization that a great deal of time has passed since the detonations occurred. Roughly 1,314,900 adannus would be required for radiation levels to be in their current range, while allowing plant life to once more thrive. This is disturbing. I now question why this fact is disturbing, yet the annihilation of an entire facility, and town, are not. It does not seem logical. Perhaps this is another side effect of my programming being somewhat askew.

The sun begins to wane. My power cells register 60%, and I find that I have discovered nothing even remotely promising that approaches a power source. *Baltu* was a veritable remnant smear upon the landscape, and I now grow concerned that further established population or military centers may be as well. This is not conducive to my continued ability to ambulate, so I cease doing so. I switch into power save mode to reconsider my initial decision, while seeking a better alternative.

117

Point zero-zero-zero-zero-two-four adannus later, I have reached a decision. While a photovoltaic attachment would still be the ideal solution to my ever-more prominent power issue, I now find the likelihood of making the journey required to obtain one less promising. Having run the statistics, I find a 72% probability of Sub-base 27 being either gone or, at the very least, in significant ruin. Further, if all population centers are annihilated, as *Baltu* was, there is a near-zero probability of finding functional power sources that I may utilize. I find myself experiencing something, so I run another diagnostic before ambulating anew.

♦　　♦　　♦　　♦　　♦

Diagnostics indicate that all is functioning in the same manner as during the prior diagnostic. Trepidation sets in, as I try to quantify my fear. Something is clearly amiss, not the least of which is that I believe that I am experiencing both trepidation and fear. This is the anomaly that I continue to attempt to isolate. This should not be possible. These are human emotions, and I am incapable of emotions. Nevertheless, these 'feelings' remain, pervasive, and in the fore of my processing cycles. For the moment, I will attempt to isolate them.

I have decided to ambulate west. From my current estimated position, which is bolstered by my initial gimbal calibration and log of strides and their lengths from my initial point of embarkation, I should reach the first outlying Aksu population center - *Saptu* - in six adannus. This decision was reached on the 49% probability that this population center will remain in-tact, either in full, or as a remnant, not directly affected by the pre-supposed war. It could still be that the 'war' was one-sided - an effort to wipe out, or significantly cripple, the capabilities of the Abanyarahhu by the Aksu. Also, it is a small population center, so it would not register as a primary target

- either in a first strike, or a retaliatory capacity - as others present a far greater, more meaningful, and ominous threat.

Ambulating to the end of the meadow, I enter a skeletal forest of deciduous trees. These are surrounded, at slightly higher elevations, by coniferous trees, upon knolls scattered at random within. At their gaunt bases, heartier vines and weeds have begun to make a comfortable home for themselves, unconcerned by the sea of death which surrounds them. I find it beautiful that something so vibrant and alive can find solace and peace - a home - in the remnants of something so abhorrent and vile. I find myself running a third diagnostic, in an effort to root out the source of the errant code that is causing me to acknowledge the subjective condition of 'beauty'. Beauty, by definition, is found only in the perceptions of the beholder(s). I am becoming concerned for the stability of my code, in and of itself, an anomaly.

Darkness falls in earnest.

Weeds and vines embrace me, and then encumber me, as I move through the confines of the arboreal wraith that is this place. This place is called *Shuruppak Forest*, if my locational calculations are at all accurate. It was once a preserve for nature, dividing the Abanyarahhu and Aksu nations. At further extremes, it forms a hilly mountain chain, which also served as a natural divider between nations.

How the nations began, no one is certain. Oral histories go back trillions of adannus, but written ones only began 26,298,000 adannus ago. Tradition that is commonly agreed upon states that Ilu, the Great Builder, placed life upon either side of this hilly range - one group to populate the east, and one the west. The Holy scriptures read thus:

"And he that created everything that we are, from the nothing we were, chose to see this land flourish with the goodness of life.

To the east, the Abanyarahhu, tillers of the land and guardians of its gifts and mercies.

To the west, the Aksu, stewards of the forests and fens, caretakers of the great balance.

To the Abanyarahhu, knowledge of the heavens, and their meanings.

To the Aksu, skill in the traversing of water.

And let both, when the proper time comes to pass, share their knowledge. And in doing so grow ever closer to Ilu, and find their way to his holy mountain in the passing of their lives from this world to the next."

119

This was only an interpretation, of course. The original tongues died long ago, or merged with the current derivations found within a populous divided by land. No one is certain when the two populations recognized the existence of the other in earnest, but trade had been occurring since prior to the written word being documented for the sake of future generations. At first, there was great jubilation: the scriptures that both nations possessed matched one another very closely. More than likely, this was simply a progressive aberration of oral tradition breaking down as the tale of Ilu was passed from generation to generation.

Trade flourished and, in time, intermarrying even became common. There were no formal borders ever claimed, save the forest through which I now ambulate and the hilly mountains upon whose spine this forest rests itself. The two nations treated this as hallowed ground, sacred to both and claimed by neither.

Over generations, science and exploration began to take hold. Population centers began to arise, and nomadic behavior dwindled to the point of either randomness, or complete obsolescence. Physics, mathematics, writing, building, architecture, the fine arts, and everything that one could conceive of advancing a society came to bear, first as a trickle and then as a torrent. Data flowed freely from one side of the hilly mountains to the other. Telecommunications developed, and power and communications lines were strung through the forest, with appropriate reverence and minimal interference. This, I believe, was the harbinger of the ill winds that followed.

As communications progressed, data became less and less a shared commodity. While the lands and oceans proved abundant with food, wood, and natural resources, data became a commodity which could strike a sizeable imbalance. As the flow of data constrained itself to a slip of its former self, it became evident to the leaders of each nation that they now had something to protect; something the other nation did not share in common. Data, then, became a stock in trade.

Militaries began to be formed, first for protection and then for offense. With these having been successfully enacted, espionage programs soon logically followed. Espionage begat counter-espionage, and as an overt warning to the opposing nation, spies were hanged in public ceremonies which were filmed and, later - as the need became apparent - broadcast. The forest and hilly mountain range, once considered sacred, was now declared a no-man's land. It was a line in the proverbial sand that was not to be crossed. Check points were established. Fences were erected. Secondary and tertiary defense measures were taken to discourage, and moreover prevent, intrusion of any kind.

The race for space became no longer about exploration, but about militarization. Telecommunications advanced and, for the first time, the populations of both nations got a glimpse of the planet that they occupied. All was open water, except to the north. In the north stood one phenomenal land mass, though it was clear that it was not only well-frozen, but being substantively riven in a number of places at the pace of a geological crawl.

Exploration, once encouraged, was now halted in an effort to divert all resources to defense. Once defense that was deemed to be adequate was in place, offense became the paramount consideration once more. With each breakthrough in offense, a defense was devised, only to lead to a new offense. The rest of the world would have to wait to be explored - there simply weren't the resources to do so during this period of antisocial development.

Ahead, I could see the beginnings of a downward slope. The forest was thicker here, though the trees were no less dead. The vines and weeds were more prolific, causing a great mass of arboreal strangulation. I hacked through the flora as strategically as I could, as I noted for the first time the birds, insects, and animals, notable in their utter absence, and this only.

Adannus came and went, until I finally reached a demonstrable parting of the choking plant life, opening into a similar meadow. On this side, the fences remained intact. I found myself losing more time in dealing with the destruction of them, in an effort to provide myself ingress into the lands of the Aksu.

Stepping through the second fence, sprawled before me, lay the Aksu valley. My first impression was that it looked markedly similar to the opposing side. However, as I ambulated across the plain, differences began to spring to the fore. There was a meandering stream, clotted with debris and bounded by abundant weeds. The dead ghosts of an orchard could be seen in the distance, standing like silent, arboreal tombstones to mark the dead in a battle that should never have been. It was then that I knew for certain that both sides had been struck; one to the other. This devastation, this ruin, was not singular to one nation. Rather, it was a perverse twining of their former selves in that it was something which they both shared. I wondered how long it had been since they had possessed something in shared commonality on this grand a scale.

'*Too long*', my subconscious mind muttered, '*Far, far too long.*'

I ran a fourth diagnostic.

The haze of clouds fade as the night takes charge of the heavens above. I see distant stars winking into existence. First the largest, followed closely by distant cousins and less luminous nephews, as well as other heavenly bodies. For a moment, I just stop, and stare, amazed at their audacity, and the stirring reverence that it demands of me. I feel...moved.

I run a fifth diagnostic.

Coming once more to my senses, I see the moon as it edges over a copse of gnarled, dead trees in the distance to my left. It is a waxing moon. Soon it will be back to its full glisten of titanium white. I wonder whether I will be under power, in order to see it do so. My probability engine kicks in once more, unbidden. I do not appreciate it, especially when I am presented with the odds. Suffice it to say, they are not in my favor.

I ambulate on. A pair of adannus pass, and as I clear a copse of what used to be fruit trees, I am able to see the population center. The first thing that I recognize is that it still retains upright structures. This is encouraging. As I continue upon my path toward potential electrical salvation, I find myself hoping for someone - anyone - to be found alive there. For the first time, I feel alone.

I run a sixth diagnostic.

Growing closer, I see not a living thing moving. I once more check my hilams meter, and it registers 682. This is once more indicative of fallout, and in all probability eliminates entirely my chances of finding sustained life within the confines.

Entering the periphery, I find paved roadways still semi-intact. These I use to ambulate more regularly, in an effort to save energy. Skeletal remains are found in random places and quantities. On occasion, I find a random animal skeleton lying about as well. The storefronts all are overgrown with a similar type of choking weed as those that I left behind in the forest. Within their display windows sun bleached items and displays remain, but they are so blasted with solar radiation as to be entirely unrecognizable. I find a storefront that appears to have been used as a motorized vehicle repair shop. I enter the confines in the hopes of finding a battery upon which to leach some much needed energy. After a few moments of furtive searching, I find a rack of thirty automotive batteries. All, however, are eaten through, exploded, or non-functioning. There is no power to be had here, then. My probability engine recalculates, and I begin to panic anew.

This time, I don't bother with the diagnostic. I know what results it will return. I am functioning properly, yet I am not.

Ambulating from the confines of the shop, I consider my final moments with Ana Rebu. Perhaps the action that he performed within my torso, prior to his failed attempt to give me the complete historical record of both nations for posterity, has something to do with my new-found expressions of human behavior? Considering this, I run a different diagnostic to test all of my expansion ports. None should be in use, yet I find that, in fact, two are. One contains a card that imbues me with an ability to utilize ultraviolet light waves for sight. This proves of no use to me, so I return it to dormancy. The other, however, is powered and actively engaged. Even so, it is running in a cloaked mode of some sort that I am not familiar with. Nor is the card identified in any way. It simply is. I could pull it out, but before I am permitted to consider the matter further, my probability engine disgorges yet another statistic: there is a 99.9999% chance that this card is what is imbuing me with these otherwise foreign traits. I fail to understand this, but I leave it in place. I might turn it off, but there seems to be no way for me to do so, as there ought to be. Further, I find that I am prevented from accessing my torso hatch. This is also curious, as it should be freely accessible. Fortunately, my power couplers are redundant, and found in my thigh hatches as well. This provides me small relief.

I spend the remainder of the night, into the early dawn, seeking batteries, the ingredients to make a rudimentary one, or anything that may provide power. I do find two petroleum distillate powered generators, but both are so decrepit and weather-beaten that I deem them irreparable. My power, for whatever reason, has also begun to diminish far faster than would be expected. As I consider this, I find it amazing that my batteries are working at all. Based on my findings, I am a bipedal miracle. I should not be under power at all, and yet here I am.

My battery power registers at a mere 23%. I choose to leave the town behind, in an attempt to make it to the next population center - *Lalartu*. It is located some four adannus away on foot, and will require 97% of my power to reach, excluding leaching. Logically, I should find safe harbor in one of the more well-constructed buildings in town, and await reactivation at a further date. But I call into question by whom, and when? Will it even be possible? With a suddenness, I recognize the curse that I have been given. I am sentient, I am utterly alone, and I am dying.

I choose instead to hold on to the thread of life, rather than doing what is rational - what I ought to do. As such, I resume ambulation toward *Lalartu*. As I ambulate, I search my databases for something - anything - that could potentially stave off the inevitable. Even after octillions of computational cycles, I arrive at no solution.

While ambulating, I disconnect my rational mind, and begin to consider what it means to be in my position.

Am I alive?

Clearly, I am not flesh and blood. So, therefore, I am not alive. But does not the presence of independent thought serve as a marker for life? If this is the criteria - independent thought - then I most certainly am alive. This thought makes me angry, as I consider the desolation around me, this man-made apocalypse. How wondrous a thing to be alive, and yet how nonchalantly that gift is squandered. Look at the disaster that the two nations made of one another. And to what end? Mutual destruction. Annihilation in the name of vanity, superiority, egotism.

I now believe myself to be the only living thing left. I am something that was built for war, and never intended to be truly alive. I - and I alone – remain. And yet in the cruelest of ironies, the humans who brought all of this into being have sealed my fate from far beyond their long-established, makeshift graves. I am dying, and I cannot extrapolate nor locate the means to save myself. Worse, I find myself wanting to live.

How could a humanity imbued with this fervor for life simply let it slip away so heinously, so flippantly?

My reverie of vilification is interrupted by a warning. I am now reduced to a scant 2% battery power, and my knee servos, which have been compensating for the #34 - left knee, camber right, non-functioning one are now failing. I am stuck in place, like a stalwart statue. A statue upon whom birds will never roost. As the sun reaches for the peak of the sky, I do what I still have the power within me to choose to do. I look all around me at the beauty that once was. I implore whatever deity that may be listening that I be allowed to live, that I be permitted the privilege to bear witness to a day when humanity finds a way to return. I dump all of these temporary cache memories to my permanent solid-state memory, and hope that someday...som...

<Entering Re-Boot Mode>

Present Day - Thiel, Antarctica

"We're nearly there," Kevin said, to his Captain.

"We ought to be," Captain Stacey retorted. "We've been drilling this hole for a God-damned eternity."

A slight lurch of the rig told the men that they had finally breached. Whatever was down there, they were going to be the first to see it since ice last receded from the Antarctic landscape some 14,000 years ago.

"Bring that fiber optic on over, Joey. We're pulling the bit now, and then we'll be ready for it."

Joey would just as soon tell him to bugger off. It was colder than a well digger's bum out here, and his snot had gone from treacle to glass. Why anyone in their right mind would expend the sort of resources Stacey had for a random anomaly - probably nothing, in fact - was absurd to him. Still, he had signed on to this expedition because it offered the one thing that remaining at home instead had not. Money. "Aye, I'll wheel it over when you're about done pulled."

It could be that Kevin nodded. It could also just as easily be that he had flipped him the bird. That was the funny thing about the Antarctic wind, and the incessant blowing frass of snow; it made communication a constant guessing game.

Over the next hour, the sections of drill were moved, twenty feet at a go. The cores were being un-sleeved by the research team from Norway, for later study in a new program. It was a program which had only recently received an obscene amount of money from a rich, and beyond eccentric, patron.

Why couldn't those blokes just give ol' Joey a little bit of that scratch, hey? Nope, puppies, and wetlands, and buggering ice in the bleeding cold - that's where those ducats went. Piss-poor choice, but it was paying his bills at the moment, he supposed.

As the last section of bit pipe was removed, the bit was once more revealed. Joey made a bee-line through the ludicrously windy conditions, into the three-sided tent with the open top flap housing the freshly drilled hole.

"Gentlemen," Stacey said, "A toast to success!"

Joey knew that he shouldn't say it, but he was cold in places he ought not to be. "Inn'int a toast usually accompanied by some, oh, I don't know, spirits of some kind, hey?"

"Now, Joey," the old salt responded, sarcasm rolling right on by him in a way that the grim reaper would certainly not in the near-term, "You know the rules."

A big stupid grin begat a big stupid grin in return, "Wanker," Joey said under his breath.

Kevin paid out the fiber optic camera. It took nearly ten minutes for it to reach bottom, and another six to get it attached to the viewing unit. It had been insulated well, but in this place 'well' was never 'well *enough*'.

The screen took eons to load. Finally, a dim wisp of light could be made out. At first the team thought something was wrong with the camera. As they adjusted the focus, it became clear to them all what they were looking at. It was metal. And it had what looked a great deal like articulated servo motors and cylinders.

THAT THING IN THE HALL

KARNA TECLA

Martin hung his car keys on the hook next to the back door. No one greeted him.

"Mom?" His voice filled the silent house. "Madeline?" he tried.

"Living room!" The frail voice was faint, but there was no family din to drown her out this afternoon.

Martin shook his head. This must be one of those days when his mother thought that his father was still alive.

"It's me, Mom. Martin. Your son." Martin leaned over the couch and kissed her. "How's your day?" He continued through the living room to put his briefcase in his home office. Even though it was Saturday, and he had gone in to the office, he still had more work to do before the trial started on Monday.

"Shh! THEY'll be coming after IT, you know."

He shut the office door. "What?" He had thought he had heard her correctly, but he wasn't sure. Martin was never sure anymore.

"THEY'll be coming after IT, you know."

He looked at his mother sitting on the couch. He thought he saw terror in her eyes. In her lap, a weapon. And on the television screen the 'I haven't touched the remote in a long time' blue.

"Mom? Are you okay?" Martin sat down next to her, and she tightened her grip on the weapon. "What are you doing with my Ghost Busters' gun?"

Timmy, his five year old, had found the relic in the basement a couple of weeks ago and had begged to play with it.

She turned to look at Martin. "Protection."

Thinking she must have heard something outside, Martin got up to check the windows, doors, and security system. Finding nothing amiss, he returned to his mother's side. "Protection from what, Mom?"

"From that THING. I was going to my room to take a nap and there IT was. IT was dead in the hall when I found IT, but THEY'll come after IT. THEY always do. THEY always come after THEIR own. I left IT there - in the hall – so THEY don't come after *me*."

Martin shook his head. "Where'd Sally take the kids?" Martin asked, hoping that a change of subject would snap his mother out of this hallucination.

"THEY took Sally and the kids. The dog, too. The dead one might still be in the hall. THEY might be back for you and me."

Martin rolled his eyes. He would never become accustomed to his mother's hallucinations and forgetfulness. The doctors had convinced Martin that his mother was no longer competent enough to take care of herself after she forgot the pumpkin pie in the oven and started a fire. Martin had been ready to place her in a care facility, but Sally, his wife, had insisted that Madeline move in with the family. Family should care for family. And that if they worked together, they could handle this. That was two years ago. Now his mother's hallucinations were a daily affair.

"Can I go check, Mom?" It was safer to play along with her. Most of the time when he tried to tell her it was all in her head, she became very agitated.

"Just you be safe, sonny. If HIS kind have come to get HIM, I don't want THEM to get you, too."

"How 'bout you give me the gun for my protection?" She released her grip as he took the pop gun off her lap. "If IT's gone, I'll come back and we can check the hall together."

She nodded.

Martin walked slowly out of the living room and through the kitchen. A short hall led from the kitchen to the mother-in-law addition they had added.

There IT was. Still lying there. In the hall. On the floor. In front of her bedroom door.

Martin returned to the kitchen. A note on the refrigerator informed him that his wife had gone to pick up the kids from swim practice. Setting the gun on the table, Martin searched around for a plastic container. It was now clear to him what had happened. Timmy must have left the cage open again and Vincent, his pet tarantula, must have escaped. Then, when Timmy left with his mother and sister, he must have been wearing the tarantula t-shirt he got from the museum.

Mom was right about one thing, though. It was dead. Martin used the lid to ease the spider into the container. Timmy would want to bury it in the back yard. As Martin returned to reassure his mother that all was good, he made a mental note that movies like *Arachnid* should not be watched when his mother was awake.

BELLE OF THE ARTS

TIM HUGHES

Editor's note: In an effort to preserve the author's original stanzas, this work's font size has been reduced to accommodate.

On a secluded city side street there rises a lion-colored brick building
sequestered by leafy shadows,
a dwelling snug in the shambling eloquence of bygone days
yet beyond its doors is revealed a world of art blaze
where you preside supreme in that ever flowing, ever thriving scene
brought forth by brush strokes from works of artists whose efforts found enhancement
all due to your instructional enchantment
as you captain their boat pass studio walls alive with each artist's glowing work,
pass every canvas islet
and you, their ever knowledgeable pilot,
at the helm as you sail an aesthetic sea
of Renaissance and Parisian beauty
your eyes dancing with Botticellian mystique,
belle of artfully sculptured features,
and golden hair like nature's alluring headdress,
a painter's dream,
so sensual, so self-commanding, so complete!

WINNEBAGO COUNTY POOR FARM

KATHI KRESOL

136

In the mid 1800's Winnebago County realized the need to deal with the issues of those individuals who were not able to support themselves, and those deemed insane. Their solution was to develop a working farm that would be sustained by its own crops, grown by the people housed at the farm. The Winnebago County Board of Supervisors voted to look for available land for purchase in 1853. It was decided to buy the farm of John DeGroot, located on Elmwood Road. The need for housing was a problem almost immediately when a cholera outbreak filled the small farmhouse to capacity. The County Board decided to move the house to land located on North Main Street at the present day site of the River Bluff Nursing Home.

This was a time when services for the mentally ill consisted of confining them, not caring for them. The conditions under which they lived was no better than if they were animals. During warm weather, the completely insane were kept in a 'stockade' that was open to the elements. During inclement weather and colder temperatures, they were penned in cells that were placed near the kitchen wall. When the temperatures rose, the stench that came from these inmates was "unhealthy and unbearable".

In the fall of 1856, there were forty-nine people served by the farm during the year. Eight of the residents died. It was decided that the county would place a 'potter's field' cemetery in back of the property. At first, only the inmates who passed away were laid to rest behind the building. Later, it would be expanded to include unidentified transients, suicides, and those who could not afford a "proper funeral".

In the fall of 1861, the farm served thirty-nine persons, six of whom were insane. Three of these had to be confined. Wadley Favor was employed as Superintendent of the farm during this time. The Winnebago County Board of Supervisors would arrange annual visits to the home to make sure the 'clients' were properly cared for. These visits were usually a big deal, and were held with "much fanfare".

The County Board granted permission in 1863 for an annex, and the next year a twenty-two-foot square outbuilding was built with an eight foot ceiling. It housed, according to the records, "three insane persons, two raving lunatics, and one entirely naked man whom it is impossible to keep clothed". Other reports from 1863

137

state that the main building housed thirty-six inmates. The farm was, by this time, self-sustaining, raising its own crops and livestock.

In 1873, a newspaper article includes a description of the poor house at this time:

"A frame building that had two stories 26 by 40 feet that housed 21 cells and a bathroom."

An article in 1875 stated that the Superintendent of the time, George Weaver, visited the Elgin Asylum to see if they had any openings for insane patients. The Superintendent of the Elgin facility refused Weaver's request, explaining that Winnebago County had a quota of twelve for insane patients and that they had already exceeded their limit and sent twenty. He explained that Winnebago County had a "larger proportion of insane persons than any other county in the state". The county sent twenty insane persons to be held at Elgin, and there were nine more confined at the poor farm.

In 1883, a new two-story building was built, and named the Winnebago County Almshouse. It used a "brick veneer to cover a wooden frame". The day of March 5, 1884 began with bitter cold temperatures. Even that was not enough to discourage an astounding six-hundred people that arrived to visit the brand new Almshouse. Many of them came by train from cities all over Northern Illinois. Sleighs were there to meet the trains, which served to take the visitors the rest of the way to the home from the depot. Visitors were said to have been very impressed with the ornately decorated reception rooms with chandeliers and carpets. The 'cells', as they had previously been labeled, were now referred to as 'apartments', and were plainly, but nicely, furnished.

The State's Attorney, Mr. Works, was introduced, and proudly announced to the crowd that the new building was considered by experts to be "the best constructed public building in the state of Illinois", according to the local newspapers of the day. Works called it a "glowing tribute", and stated that it should make people proud that such a wonderful place was made for the poor and homeless.

Superintendent Sam Jones spoke next, and stated that though at one time the Winnebago County facility was once considered "the worst in Illinois", this new building would serve as a new beginning. He spoke of the Board's visits to other almshouses in the state, and choosing one to use as a model. Jones promised that this new house would serve anyone who needed help despite color, age, or religious persuasion. Most who visited that day agreed it was a wonderful "haven" for the county's indigent. The paper titled the article "Pauper's Palace".

In 1893, Alexander Collier was the Superintendent of the Almshouse. There were sixty-four inmates on the two-hundred acre farm. One great advantage of the new building, built in 1883, was that the violently insane were separated from the other patients.

In November of 1904, the almshouse was found to be in poor condition. The newspapers claimed it was dirty, dingy, and not fit for *anyone* to live in. In 1905, it was decided that the insane patients would be transferred to the Bartonville Insane Asylum. The County Board also decided to listen to Dr. Crawford at the Almshouse, and create a sick ward at the poor farm that would include an operating room. The emphasis of the new ward would be the medical treatment of Rockford's poor. In 1907, an inspection showed the almshouse to be greatly improved, with a separate house for any contagious diseases - something that the staff had requested for many years.

In 1919, the newspapers told the story of John Leffler. Leffler was born and raised in Rockford. Sometime around 1870, he decided to leave Rockford and see what adventures might be waiting beyond the city limits. He traveled first to Iowa, where he applied his knowledge of carpentry skills to work on the state capitol building. The promises of further riches led Leffler to travel all the way to California, where he finally settled in Los Angeles. During his travels, he lost track of his relatives in Rockford. Leffler grew older and began to reminisce about his childhood, and the family that he had left behind. He decided to return to Rockford, but he had very little money. So John Leffler, at the advanced age of eighty-seven years old, decided that he would *walk* all the way back to his hometown in Illinois. He left Los Angeles and, when his money ran out, he was able to live off of the kindness of strangers. Leffler walked over the mountains, across rivers, and over plains until he reached Kansas City.

Unfortunately, it was here that Leffler ran into disaster. He was walking along the railroad tracks when he was struck by a train. The police ambulance took him to the hospital where it was decided that his leg needed to be amputated. Leffler shared his story of his quest to reach Rockford with the nurses and doctors. They were all very touched by his tale, and together decided to help the old man. They put him on a train to Rockford, and made arrangements through the local Traveler's Aid Society have a representative meet him at the train station when he arrived.

Leffler was picked up as planned by a representative of the Society, who also found him short term lodging while the Overseer of the Poor, George Wilson, assisted in searching for Leffler's family. Unfortunately, George searched in vain. In the end, it was decided that Leffler be admitted to the Almshouse in 1919. He remained in residence there until his death.

In July of 1930, the Winnebago County Almshouse got a new look. Superintendent Conklin told a Rockford Republic reporter that all eighty of their beds were filled. He went on to explain that they had to turn some very needy people away because they just "could not care for anymore".

During this time, the back of the building was used as a county hospital. It added thirty beds, and the facility was once again called the Winnebago County Poor Farm. The county finally voted to expand the building portion, and construction was begun soon after on the 136' x 32' wide addition. It would provide the home with a much needed hospital that would house one-hundred additional beds.

The 'farm' was still just that - a working farm that included 147 acres that was owned by the county, and an additional 137 acres that the county rented. There were also 157 hogs and heads of cattle, and 47 sheep. The 'inmates' that were able to work helped with tending to both the animals and the crops.

Tucked behind the new building, closer to the tree line, was the Winnebago County Poor Farm Cemetery. Essentially, it was the county's potter's field. Prior to 1885, the potter's field was found on Owen Center Road, two miles northwest of the new location. In that year, the bodies were all moved to the quiet spot along the Rock River. They had markers during the 1930's, but most of them contained numbers instead of names.

"Few people ever visit the potter's field and no flowers cover the graves. No one ever stops there in search of the grave of a loved one. Those buried in the potter's field are truly forgotten," Superintendent Conklin stated.

Rising adjacent to the present buildings at the Winnebago county farm is a new and model county hospital which will rise three stories, cost $50,000 and contain 100 beds. It will be one of the outstanding county hospitals in downstate Illinois.

From the July 20, 1930 Register Republic.
(Used with permission from The Rockford Register Star & rrstar.com)

By 1932, the Winnebago County Poor Farm was in dire financial straits. Smaller townships in the surrounding area agreed to pay the farm for providing care for their poor, and then failed to follow through with their part of the bargain. They were behind by almost $45,000. They estimated an operating overhead cost of just over $.70 per patient, per day, for those in the home, and almost $2.00 per patient, per day, for those in the hospital. An average day at the farm saw over 100 patients in the home, plus another 35 in the hospital. Those patients who were physically able helped with whatever farming or housekeeping chores that required doing. But many of the inmates were too sick, or too old, to be of much assistance.

Polio hit Rockford hard in the summer of 1945. In a four month period, 382 cases were reported statewide. Of these, 194 were reported in Winnebago County. Most of those patients were treated at the County Hospital. The peak occurred during the week of August 5 to August 13, when 57 people were stricken. During that summer, 36 people died from the outbreak, most of them children. Nurses were brought in from all over the country to help with the patients and, at the peak, over 200 of them worked at the County Hospital.

The worst cases were contained at the County Hospital, including the patients who required the iron lung machines to help them breathe. An office was set up in the Faust Hotel, where families could receive updated information. This was necessary due to the need to quarantine the patients.

There was a special Polio Committee formed to help with the epidemic. It released warnings to parents to keep their children at home and away from the pools, theaters, playgrounds - anywhere they would be around other children. The committee also made requests of the community for blankets, doctor's gowns, and other items.

Other nurses visited the individuals who were stricken with less severe cases. Their role was to check on the patients, and their families. These nurses were sometimes accompanied by a food inspector.

In 1945, doctors were not certain what caused polio. They had no idea why that particular year was so bad. The summer of 1945 had twice the number of polio cases than the year before. Dichlorodiphenyltrichloroethane pesticides (more commonly known as 'DDT') were used around the eight different milk pasteurization plants and the hospitals. The spraying was suggested to help cut down the number of flies. Proper garbage handling was also emphasized. The DDT was sprayed from big trucks with thirty hand pumps.

A ban was put on high school sports in the fall of 1945, while authorities tried to get the situation under control. Other towns, such as Freeport, took the drastic measure of closing theaters and other places where people would gather in groups.

Rockford struggled with the polio issue for years, until Jonas Salk's vaccine arrived in 1955. Cases of the disease never again grew to the numbers that were experienced in 1945. Later, people, as well as the newspapers, would refer to that year as the "Summer of Fear".

By 1949, the financial struggles to keep the hospital and home operational caused the County to consider at other options. The idea that the county selected was to turn the poor home portion of the farm into a nursing home. This plan would shift the burden of responsibility from the township to the state. The land portion was still used as a farm, and continued to play host to livestock.

In the later part of the 1950's, the decision was made to use the farm to grow crops to feed the on-site livestock. The livestock, in turn, would be used to supply the milk and meat for the nursing home. This decision would reunite the two entities for the first time in five years. Previously, the County Farm and the County Home for the Poor were conducted jointly for over seventy years until 1953 when they were separated. In the 1960's, the livestock was sold off and the County entertained the idea of turning the farm portion of the land into the River Bluff Forest Preserve. That idea was eventually rejected.

In 1966, Elsie Bickford a resident of River Bluff Nursing Home passed away. She had lived at River Bluff for 76 years. Elsie was only eleven years old when her grandmother, who had raised Elsie since the deaths of her parents, became too ill to care for her. Elsie moved to the Winnebago County Poor Farm on May 15, 1889. At the time Elsie came to the home, there were other children living there. One by one, each of the other children went to live with families until Elsie was the only child left at the home. When she became an adult, Elsie continued to live at the Farm, though whether this was because of employment or not was never explained. She worked in the laundry. Then, eventually, other jobs were added. Elsie passed away on April 14, 1966 at the age of 87 years old.

In 1968, a referendum was passed to build a replacement for the 80-year-old building that had, once again, grown dangerously overcrowded. The old building was filled with 204 patients, with another 70 on the waiting list. The beautiful new building was opened in 1971. It continues to care for elderly patients needs to this day - whether it be rehabilitation, so that they can return home after an illness or surgery, or for long term care.

The Winnebago County Poor Farm Cemetery fell into neglect, especially since the last burial in 1953. Weeds covered the stones. Many of the graves were vandalized. One young man, Michael Spring, worked on the cemetery for a while, trying to cut back the grass and mend the broken tombstones. Michael was a member of the Scout Troop 424, and had elected to work on the cemetery as part of an Eagle Scout project.

In a grove of sturdy trees above the river lies God's acre, where the unnamed and unfortunate are buried. Far from being a gruesome place, however, the little burial ground is a restful grove in the full flood of summer, with the wind sighing in the trees and the blue river glimpsed through their trunks in the distance.

From the July 20, 1930 Register Republic.
(Used with permission from The Rockford Register Star & rrstar.com)

Eventually, it was decided to remove the remaining stones and place a memorial marker for the over 600 men, women, and children that were buried there. The stone was placed just off a nicely paved path that runs behind the present day River Bluff Nursing Home. It serves as a reminder that many in our community who struggled to provide for their loved ones, because of illness or financial difficulties, were cared for by the facility and laid to rest here in this peaceful spot. The plaque, designed by Dick Farrell's Forest Hills Monument Company, was dedicated on June 22, 1973. It states:

IN MEMORIAM
MORE THAN SIX HUNDRED MEN
WOMEN AND CHILDREN WERE INTERRED
IN THIS GROUND FROM THE YEAR
1884 THROUGH 1954.

TO THE MEMORY OF THOSE KNOWN
AND UNKNOWN WHO LIE BURIED HERE.
THIS MEMORIAL IS REVERENTLY
DEDICATED BY
THE WINNEBAGO COUNTY BOARD
~ 1973 ~

Two Old Friends

Karna Tecla

Hiking around the lake
I discovered them.
Two old friends
Sunning themselves by the shore,
Momentarily abandoned by their owner, cooling in a swim.

Their soles full of pride in their owner –
Their tongues spoke volumes:
Of basketball games played on the corner court
Of hurdles jumped and races won
Of hikes for miles and long bike rides

I waved
At the owner,
And pressed on around the lake,
Wondering what my sneaks
Would eventually say
About me.

148

EXPONENTIAL

HEATH D. ALBERTS

150

I had been a dealer in rare books for decades when I first came upon the one that would change my life. It wasn't a self-help book in the traditional sense. Nor was it a diet book, a memoir, a cookbook, or even one based in psychology, religion, or sociology. No, the book I found was something far darker in nature.

As I write these words, I consider my actions. I wonder who will read this, or if anyone ever will at all. Perhaps others in the distant past have found themselves in my present position, though I can't wrap my head around how that might be so. I can't believe anyone else would have had the audacity to take things to the extremes which I have.

The fates of the book and myself first intertwined at a stall at the *California International Antiquarian Book Fair*. The stall was run by a reputable dealer in incunabulum whose home territory was in the United Arab Emirates, but whose sales and renown spanned the globe. His sales were often masterstrokes of connectivity between buyer and seller. Some of those sales took months to broker, but he possessed the singular skill, patience, and understanding to make them occur just the same.

Over the decade or so preceding my procurement of the work from him, we had developed a loose friendship. I would bump into him at fairs from time to time, and we found that we had much in common. We were both fans of Arsenal, for starters. A fact that seemed improbable considering that he was born and raised in the UAE, and I in Toronto. Nevertheless, that single choice to wear my Arsenal jersey to a fair changed the course of my life forever.

My specialty, much to the chagrin of my wallet and bank account, was dealing in unique works of the occult, especially those of early mass publication. The older the better. Though seldom did a tome of note that was exceedingly old come on offer that I could either afford in the first place, or that didn't have a private buyer lined up already. Still, I managed to carve out my niche with what I could get my hands on, all while connecting with sellers and buyers that were advantageous to know.

So when this particular dealer had made mention of the severe injury of an Arsenal player, I found myself curious, encouraged to take the conversational bait. That was how our friendship began.

On this day, some ten years later, I rounded the corner of one of numerous aisles. This time, I was seeking him out to say a face-to-face hello, and catch up with him as his time permitted.

I was not disappointed. As I approached, he had seen me coming, Arsenal jersey a flaming red beacon in his peripheral vision. His head turned my way, with a knowing smile already spreading across his handsome middle-eastern features.

"My friend!" he bellowed, indifferent to how those around him might react to his volume.

While flattered by the devil-may-care geniality of the greeting, I was too self-aware to ever do such a thing. I simply smiled and waved. "How are things?" I asked, when I stood before him, and his open-concept booth.

"They're good on some days, and not so good on others," was his generic reply. "And yourself?"

I was in the midst of being blown away by his booth, so it took me a beat or two longer than I would have liked to answer. "I'm getting by, and doing what I love."

"That is enough, then," he said, with a satisfied nod.

"I see that things have been more good than bad for you," I offered, spreading my hands wide to indicate his near museum quality set up. It was the poshest I had yet seen, and I had walked two-thirds of the show already.

In a moment of genuine humility, he toned his response down, "It is only a workspace that caters to my clientele's expectations."

"Anything interesting since we last spoke?" I asked. I knew better than to ask for two reasons. First, because whatever inventory he had I could never begin to afford. Second, because the tug of a second smile was his tell. If my read on him were any indicator, he not only had something, he had something that he was proud of, and eager to show me.

"It is fortuitous that you should ask," he replied, permitting the smile to come fully into the world at large. He strode over to one of the central cases, a hexagonal marvel of crystal shelves and lighting that would suffice for the display of crown jewels, let alone old books. From a coiled black strap at his wrist he selected the appropriate key, fitting it into a lock in the pedestal. An imperceptible door clicked open, revealing a storage space. From within, he reverently removed a clamshell box, done all in royal purple.

I was pretty sure that I heard my wallet scream and faint.

After locking the pedestal anew, he moved to a glass display counter. I took my place on the customer side as he opened the clamshell. He did so in a way that permitted him to see what was within, but prevented me from viewing anything more than the lid of the opulent box.

"You're killing me here," I suggested.

"These things are like a fine Turkish coffee. These moments in life are meant to be savored, for they are so few and far between."

I didn't necessarily disagree, but I was on a working walkabout at the massive show. And while I hoped that he would carve out some time after hours to catch up with me, there was not a great deal of time to be spent idling in his booth space. A space that my financial station should have prevented me from setting foot in in the first place without a klaxon of alarm coupled with flashing red 'intruder' lights.

His smile never wavered, and his gaze was piercing as he spun the half open box toward me.

Within I saw an unremarkable volume that looked like a good war might do thousands of dollars worth of improvements to it. It was faded, stained, and bound in some sort of animal skin. The edges of the soft cover were fringed with wear, and damage of all sorts. There was no title on the cover, nor visible markings of any sort.

"May I?" I asked.

"Of course."

From my pocket I produced a pair of archival gloves. I removed them from within their protective bag, and slid the white coverings over my hands. There were two schools of thought, in recent years, on the necessity of the gloves. My opinion fell somewhere in the middle, depending on the volume's age, materials, and ownership.

With reverence, I removed the work from the clamshell. Beneath it was a purple cloth which permitted me to place it gently upon the glass case's top. Tilting my head, I examined the spine. As with the cover, there were no indicators of any sort to hint at what might be inside.

"I see you're in the Turkish coffee zone," my friend joked, referring to my slow savoring of the work.

He was not wrong in the slightest. Some of the most heightened moments in my life had been spent like this. I hate to equate them to those short moments before sexual climax, but I cannot find a more apropos comparison. It is very much akin to that. There are a few moments leading up to what will either be a letdown in the absence of bliss in the aftermath, or a rare moment when the male orgasm lasts through multiple iterations, getting more and more intense with each passing moment. In this business, ninety-nine times out of a hundred, it was the prior.

This would be the latter, though I did not know it just then.

"What's the origin?" I inquired, as I re-cradled the book to transition from obverse to reverse.

Still nothing to indicate content.

"Masivul Bucegi, purportedly. Though I have no way to confirm it."

The name struck a chord in my mind, though it didn't click immediately.

My friend seemed to catch the hint of recognition as it fleeted across my features. "It is the mountain where the Sphinx of Bucegi and the Babele Monoliths were discovered in Romania."

"I vaguely remember something about that," I replied, turning the book over and around. My mind was waiting to register some as yet unseen hint of what I was holding. It was a fruitless endeavor.

If you're not a lover of puzzles, nor a serious collector of books (and I don't mean a person who amasses them, but a true bibliophile who holds an awe filled reverence for the things, bordering on insanity), then you might not understand the phenomena of one's desiring to puzzle out a book from stem to stern. It's sort of like savoring a fine wine. You don't just guzzle it. You sniff it. You check its legs, its color. You permit it to gloss over your tongue, and then you permit the flavor to augment by inducing air. Then, and only then, do you drink sparingly and in earnest, savoring each drop until the last. So it is with the bibliophile and their book.

"It's a mess."

"It's a beautiful mess."

"They usually are."

"Is it safe to open?"

"Indeed. It is made to a standard which I seldom see. While I would not appreciate your doing so, it could be handled just as a finely bound volume from an upscale printing house could be in the modern day. Gerhard Steidl would approve, if not wish to deconstruct it."

High praise, though I doubted that Steidl, the renowned bookbinder, would waste his time with such endeavors. He would, I reckoned, just appreciate the thing, acknowledge the craftsmanship, and get back to work. Having never met the man myself, however, it was only a hypothesis.

With the go ahead now afforded, I opened the book. There was no free endpaper. Instead, there was an immediate beginning to the work that began beside the front pastedown. The writing on the first twelve pages or so was clearly done in one hand. It was in a language that I had never seen before, though that wasn't saying much, given my limited exposure to works of this apparent age. Interspersed amongst what I presumed to be words were a number of arcane diagrams that I could not begin to parse, and one illumination which I got the basic meaning of in an instant. It was a man, holding a book. It was open before him, as he stood atop a mound of bodies. A latticework hung in the air above him, and a pit opened just at the cusp of where the final bodies ended.

A shiver went up my back. I did not know what the picture was attempting to convey to the reader, but it certainly set me to wondering.

Then, on page thirteen, the handwriting changed, and things got a bit queerer. Gone was the jagged script that had been laid down on those first twelve pages. Now, the handwriting was the same for short bursts. Sometimes it was a single line before a transition. At other times, it was page upon page of writing, line after line. At about page twenty, the writing diminished in size. By page twenty-two, the writing began running vertically over the horizontal. A page further still, and the writing crossed every which way until there was scarcely enough room to add anything further, lest the original text be lost to all recognition, heavy scrutinizing or no.

"I've never seen anything like it," I admitted.

"Nor had I," my friend concurred "Except, perhaps, personal letters written when paper was a scarce commodity."

"What language is this?"

"I did not recognize it, so I sent samples to some friends at Oxford and MIT."

When I could bear the pause no longer, I broached the silence, "And?"

"They all have varying opinions, but none could conclude with any certainty which branch of language had birthed it, or vice-versa."

"I find that a little hard to believe," I balked.

"I did as well," my friend concurred. "I thought that I might not have made my desired intentions clear, so I asked some leading questions – generalities. No one could offer any answers at all, but the individuals I spoke with promised me that they would look into it."

"I'm betting that if their passion for their work is as strong as yours or mine that they'll be all over it."

"I would think so, yes. The problem is, this was months ago. The check-ins remain constant. They all announce failure, coupled with a fervent desire to study the work further, in house, under more favorable conditions and with on-site equipment."

"What are you waiting for?" I asked, figuring there had to be a reason he hadn't pursued it.

"I'm waiting for this. For you."

"For me?" I half-shrieked, stunned by the strange revelation.

He just nodded. "I need someone to, shall we say, chaperone the book."

Before I could continue the discussion, an important client entered the stall. I know they were important, because my friend left the book in my hands, walked over to them, and greeted them as though they were the only person left in the world. It was how his clients expected to be treated, though I admit that I was a bit miffed at the brush off.

It was a full thirty-five minutes of hand-holding, feigned laughter, and narcissistic stories about a collection my friend would most likely never see, before he returned to me.

"Listen," he said, motioning for the book to be replaced in the clamshell. "Why don't you stop by my hotel this evening? We can talk more about what I'm proposing, and I'll bring the book there."

From somewhere about his person, he produced a business card and a pen that looked like it cost more than my first car. On the back he wrote a hotel name, and room number. "Drop by after eight, if that works for you."

The customer returned with another question about a book he had already been shown.

With more work to do before the show closed for the day, I ambled off. I bought nothing more that day. It ended up being a total waste, as I threaded my way around the show floor in a zombie-like haze. I could not get the bizarre book out of my mind.

◆   ◆   ◆   ◆   ◆

I wasn't in the worst hotel in town. That being said, I had to travel a full ten minutes to reach the part of town that my friend was staying in. I walked into a lobby that actually *was* opulent, not just made to look so. The concierge was not a post-pubescent college dormer, but an honest-to-God Higgins from *Magnum PI* major domo type. His passing glance told me I had just been sized up on the fly. Apparently, I made the grade to miss being interrogated or escorted via the bum's rush from the premises.

I rode the glass elevator to the twenty-second floor. Like a child watching *Sesame Street,* I counted along with the room numbers aloud (though just under my breath). My knock was answered in seconds.

"Come in!" said the first friendly face I had seen since crossing the threshold of the building.

"May I offer you something to drink?"

"No, I'm good," I said, visually absorbing the suite. The place was posh, bordering on unnecessary. The word 'utilitarian' would never be uttered while choosing to be confined here.

My friend motioned me to the quartz topped bar that fronted the full kitchen. There, upon its gleaming top, was the clamshell.

Slipping on a fresh set of archival gloves, I sat down, and returned to where I had left off with the book. Its spell was not diminished upon second viewing. In fact, it was stronger still.

"I can see that you have an affinity for the thing."

"Who among us wouldn't?"

A subtle chuckle. "Agreed."

"So, you know I can't afford this. But you mentioned 'chaperoning'."

"Right. I want to sell this book. In order to do that, and fetch top dollar, I need some things done. Testing, for starters. I need to know how old the thing is. I also need to know the language and, best case scenario, what it says or who the author or authors might have been."

"That last statement begs some question," I responded. "I'm seeing at least a dozen hands in here, and possibly more."

"I had the same thought, with an exception."

"That being?"

"That perhaps it is the same hand, but amended over the course of years, possibly decades, and also under the influence of age, intoxicants, or injury."

The thought hadn't occurred to me, which made me feel foolish. That was, until I realized why my subconscious mind had glossed over the possibility. "I'm no handwriting expert, but I'm of the mind that there's no way in hell this is the same hand. I'm just not seeing it."

'Would you stake your reputation on it?" my friend asked, cocking an accusing eye in my direction.

I blew out a sigh, "For what little that's worth? Yes. I believe that I would."

A smile played impishly on his lips, "I agree."

"I'm sorry, but when did this become homework with a pop quiz?" I was a bit flustered with his methods, and I was tired from the long day.

"I'm sorry, my friend. No harm meant," was his genial reply.

"No," I said, "I'm sorry. It's been a long day, and I'm cranky. I apologize."

"Let us focus on the book, and my proposal. I would be willing to pay you a weekly stipend, plus reimburse you for all travel costs." Then he added, "Including upgrades and incidentals."

"This book is that important to you?"

"It is, when you consider what I believe it will fetch, when authenticated."

When he quoted the price, I nearly fell off of my stool. "Holy shit! *That* much?"

"Quite possibly, or more. Yes."

When he quoted the weekly stipend he was willing to part with, I almost dropped the book. "You're nuts!"

"What I am, is determined. And in need of someone I know, and that I can trust."

"And how do you know you can trust me that well?"

"Honestly? No man knows the heart of another man fully. What I do know is that you've been with the ABAA almost since your inception. You've ridden out highs and lows in the industry, and managed to keep a customer base that speaks highly of you when I cross paths with them. You've earned the respect of your peers, and you've never once shown me anything other than kindness and friendship. So call it a gamble that I'm willing to take."

While the kind words were appreciated, I was a bit surprised to hear about clients in common. I couldn't recall a single one who had ever mentioned him to me. Then again, perhaps they were playing in the minor leagues with me, before moving up to the majors with the likes of him. I often had clients who 'fell off the radar', never to be heard from again. I'd make soft-sell attempts at contacting them, usually via e-mail, but seldom in person or over the phone. Book buyers tended to be a quiet and solitary lot (though not always, certainly). If they wanted something, and you had it on offer, they found you.

"I feel like I can't say no, here."

"The question isn't whether you can or can't. The question is, why would you?"

I couldn't think of a single reason. It was a dream assignment, and one I would probably do for free. Then again, I could always use the money. Most of my sales were done via Internet and mail order, so I had no storefront to tie me down. I had a nephew who lived near my home whom I could trust to package and mail any sales as they happened in my absence. As a college junior awash in debt, he could use the extra income. Of that I was certain.

"I can't rationalize anything other than doing this."

"Excellent!"

MIT - Five Days Later

The *Ray & Maria Stata Center* in Cambridge was the single strangest structure I had ever laid eyes on. To say that it was something out of *'Alice's Adventures in Wonderland'* wasn't quite far enough. It was a rambling mass of odd shapes, changing surface finishes, and sun-dappled chaos. It was beautiful in its ugliness. It was within those odd walls that the likes of Noam Chomsky and David Pesetsky made their second homes. In short, it was a modern-day Mecca to the spoken and written word.

While I would have liked nothing more than to have met with either of those individuals, or their peers, I found myself relegated to an escort that consisted of a single, hyper-loquacious intern named Raymond.

I was escorted to the office of an ancient and grizzled man, who stood all of four-foot-three, and looked like a diminutive, weathered tree. The door read *'Professor Balkan'*.

"Come in, dear boy, come in!" the man said, as he shuffled around his desk to shake my hand. "That will be all Raymond, thank you," he added.

"Thank you for seeing me," I opened.

"It's no trouble at all," he replied, ushering me into a chair. He took the one adjacent to it, and we found ourselves on either side of a small end table. "I'm really quite intrigued."

I took the clamshell from within my backpack, and placed it in the center of the table.

"I've had one ginny of a time trying to discern what in the nine circles of Hell it is that you have there. We've been poring over the initial photos that we received months ago, but there isn't anything like seeing the real McCoy."

"And?"

"And I've found some possibilities, but my chief one makes the least sense. Which is why I was so desperate to see the work in its entirety."

"I don't understand."

"Well you might not have noticed, but I've been around for a while."

This got a laugh out of me before I could stifle it.

My look of shock must have shown, because he shared the laugh, and said, "No need to be bashful. The truth is a beautiful thing. Someday, God willing, you'll look this way, too.

"And you know what? You'll be happy about it, because it beats the pants off of the alternative."

"On that we can agree."

"Are you familiar with the work 'The Instructions of Šuruppak'?

I admitted that I was not.

"Well, that's all right, then. Most folks aren't," he scoffed with good humor. "That book is, by all accounts, one of the first known examples of the written word. It's been dated to some time around 2600 BC. It's a cuneiform tablet, so it probably doesn't qualify as a book by your contemporary definition. Mine is a little broader, in that sense. Still, what's astounding is that the language that your book is written in feels almost like an unknown predecessor to Sumerian cuneiform."

"Which is an impossibility," I added.

"Oh? And why is that?" he asked, genuinely curious it seemed.

"Well, bookbinding, and paper and skin books, weren't prevalent until far later. Around the fifth century AD, if memory serves."

"Close enough," Balkan said, nodding. "But how do we know that someone didn't take what they knew of the old language, write something new, and then bind it? Or copy it from an original tablet, for that matter?"

This brought me up short. "I hadn't thought about it like that."

"Most don't. And that's okay. Skepticism gets better with age. As does accepting that sometimes the answer to the question is a question in itself."

"So let's say that it is a variant of ancient Sumerian. Can you decipher it?"

"I can, and I can't. Which is a stupid answer, so let me rephrase it. I can find someone who probably can, but I personally cannot, no."

"All right, so can you point me in their direction?"

"Let me see the book first, if it's all the same to you. I don't know if I'll live another day, let alone another hour, so I don't want to miss having held it."

With reverence, the Professor donned gloves, and did as I had. Everything, almost in exacting form, that I had done to and with the book he did as well. It was a full five minutes before he restored it to the clamshell. "What you have," he began, "is an extraordinary specimen of the binding craft. It is calf skin vellum, bound in calf skin leather, so it's a fairly modern book by comparison to its contents. I'd guess somewhere in the thirteenth century."

"AD?"

"AD."

"That can't be right," I responded, perplexed.

"Well, I could be wrong," the Professor assented, "but I don't believe that I'm too far off the mark.

"What I'd like to do is keep the book for a week or two. Call in a few favors, and have it looked at. Would you be amicable to that?"

"I'm sorry, but no. I just can't."

"Oh?"

"The book isn't mine. It belongs to a dealer friend of mine from the UAE. He's hired me to get it checked out, as well as figure out what it is that he's got his hands on."

"Oh, I see," Balkan said, deflating.

"But," I added, "I see no reason that you couldn't make a high resolution copy of the entire thing. X-rays, CAT scans, whatever you like. The only thing that I ask is that you keep the book on a need-to-know basis. I don't want word about this find spreading any further than it has or needs to be until it's proven to be newsworthy, authentic, or preferably both."

"I couldn't ask for more, under the circumstances," the Professor consented. "I agree."

We shook hands. It was the single most important handshake of my life. I know that now.

Two Weeks Later – 8:36 PM EST

It had been an exhausting pair of weeks. From MIT I had flown to Oxford, where I permitted another Professor to peruse the work in full for the first time. I gave him a copy of the MIT data, but insisted that if a find was made that MIT be credited as well. They had spent the time, energy, and money to scan the thing in every conceivable manner.

I did the same thing, four days later, at Stanford. I had flown over the Atlantic twice in one week. If I never had to do it again, I'd be completely fine with that.

I received an e-mail from Stanford four minutes ago. It was the first response that I had received that didn't involve just touching base for the sake of doing so. The e-mail address was a bit puzzling, so I jumped on *Google* and did some investigating. The message had been sent from an address that was designated as a part of Stanford's in-house IT department. The sender's name was Ming Ho (imagine *that* kid's problems growing up). His e-mail said he wanted to *Skype* with me, immediately, and that he would be waiting.

There was just one problem: I didn't know how in the hell to do that. I was in New York, scheduled to visit with an archaeological antiquities dealer the following morning. I didn't know what to do, so I just dug in, and called the front desk.

"Listen," I said, "I know this is going to sound weird, but can you tell me if anyone on staff knows how to *Skype*?"

"You mean," came the genial voice from the opposing end, "just use it? Or set it up?"

"Uh-"

"Do you have a computer up there?"

"I do, yes," I replied, thankful for a question, rather than laughter in response to my obvious plight.

"Okay," the voice continued, "is there a little round thing, or square thing, in the top of the lid, just above the screen?"

At first I didn't know what in the heck he meant, but lo and behold, there it was. "There is! I never paid attention to it, but there it is."

"Excellent," the man said. "If you could give me five minutes, and it wouldn't be an imposition, I'll come up and assist you in setting it up."

"That'd be great," I said, relieved. "There's a twenty in this for you, too. I appreciate the help."

"I'll be up in three minutes, then," he said, chuckling.

It was more like two minutes and some change. The fellow gave a soft knock, and I ushered him in. His dull brass name tag read 'Larry G'. I handed him the twenty, and thanked him again.

"It's no trouble."

His fingers danced over the keyboard, and I saw a screen fly past. "Was that a military caricature?" I asked, over his shoulder.

A nod as fingers continued to flutter like a hummingbird, "It's a reputable site for downloading software."

"Oh," I replied.

Moments later, a light blue *Skype* logo appeared on my screen. Now the fellow had opened a second one next to it, and was typing in Ming Ho's provided data. Something happened, and then the handsome though gaunt looking face of a young Asian man filled the center of my screen.

The fellow from the desk abdicated his space, and permitted me to replace him. A moment later he had slipped out the door.

When I looked back at the screen, Ming had a strange look on his face.

"You're probably wondering-"

"Oh, I am, but I don't want to be intrusive."

I laughed, "It's not what you think. Unless it is. Let's just say I didn't know what a '*Skype*' was until a few minutes ago. My friend Andrew Jackson helped me change all that, with the help of the concierge of the hotel here in New York."

This got the desired laugh out of him, and put him once more at ease. "I figured as much, but you never know these days."

"Anyway, your e-mail was a bit cryptic. Frankly, I was surprised to get it at all. May I ask how you're connected to the group there at Stanford?"

"Look," Ming said, after a long pause, "I'll level with you. I'm not with the group at all. I just got curious about what was up after you left. I work in IT. I was in the outer office the day you stopped by. I was offered very little by way of information, so I may or may not have come by the scan of your book by 'accident'. I'm sticking my neck way out, here."

I understood. I wasn't thrilled that we now had an interloper, but I would keep whatever he wanted private, so long as he had a lead. I told him as much.

"What you have," he offered, "is a hybrid language."

"A what?"

"It's a combination of two ancient languages. One is Sumerian. The other is a Chinese ideogram dialect."

I was skeptical. "How come no one else has figured that out, if it's that simple?"

This seemed to frustrate him. "If it were simple, someone *would* have. But it isn't simple at all. The characters are intertwined, overlaid, and interspersed. I'm not even sure how my mind managed to land on it, but when it did, I finally teased some sense out of the chaos."

"You know what it says!"

His face answered before he did. "Well, no. Not exactly, anyway. The last pages all appear to be the same. I think they're all names. It's the first twelve that have me lost. If I knew what they were, I could work backward a lot easier. Once I recognized pieces of name nomenclature in the back pages, I was able to put some things together. Even so, I can't translate exact meaning. I'm just hypothesizing that they're names."

"And you're sure about this?"

"I'm as sure as anyone else who's gotten back to you," he sniped. Then he softened, "Yeah. Pretty sure."

"You know that I'll have to share this information," I posited.

"I figured."

"So, here's what I propose. I was lost on campus, and you walked me back on course. During that walk, we talked about why I was there. I noted your curiosity and saw no harm in providing you with a copy. That sound about right?"

"It's your story," he said, grinning.

"I'll make sure you get credit, if there's any to get. Though my patron might see clear to getting in touch with you. I can't promise anything."

"I just like the challenge of the puzzle," he shot back. "If I were in this for anything else, I wouldn't have risked calling."

I believed him, but something still wasn't sitting right. Even so, I had what I wanted – a lead. I didn't care how I had gotten it. That was my focus, for the moment. As soon as we closed the connection, I was on the phone with Professor Balkan. He had given me his private cell phone number, and had promised to keep it on until we spoke again. I woke him up. It was just after 9 pm.

"No, no. No trouble. Just dozing," he said from the other end, as he got his waking bearings.

"The last pages. The ones in the other hands? They're names."

"They're...names? How did you come to know this?"

"Stanford figured it out. There's a bright kid there named Ming Ho. Apparently he's studied ideograms extensively. His take is that it's a hybridization of Sumerian cuneiform and early Chinese ideograms."

"That's preposterous," the Professor scoffed.

I could almost picture him waving the notion off, shaking his head.

"Maybe so," I pushed on, "but he seems certain that the final pages are filled with page after page of names."

"Let's say that he's right," the Professor bounced back. "Why on Earth would someone hybridize those two things? Who would take the time and effort to learn to read and write uniformly in such a manner?"

"I've given that a little thought," accent on 'little'. It was more like two minutes, but the thought had smacked me in the brain. "What if someone needed to write down names, but also wanted to keep what they were writing a secret?"

"You mean like a ledger of names?"

"Yes."

"For what purpose?"

"Who knows?

"But imagine if Hitler had done so, instead of using the names of his victims. If he were ever caught, it would provide a cover for what was really going on."

"You realize that in some cases he *did* do that – except he used numbers."

"Then you see my point," I parried.

"Well, I can't imagine why someone would want to do such-"

"The question of 'why' is a valid one. But consider that, thousands of years from now, no one would believe that Hitler would have had a reason to do something so heinous. But he did. It was done. It happened. We know why, and the answer is because he was a madman. What if we're dealing with another like him?"

"Then God help us all."

Two Days Later

Two days later, my laptop - which I had taken to leaving open and on - made a strange noise. It took me a few moments to comprehend that *Skype* was trying to get my attention, and a few more to make the connection. There, on my screen, appeared the familiar face of Ming Ho. It was after eleven pm.

"Good evening," I greeted, curious about the nature of his call so late in the evening.

"I hoped to find you awake. I hope you're not angry."

"No, it's fine. My life has become a strange series of events during which I find myself keeping abnormal hours. What may I do for you?"

"Well, I've done some digging. They're definitely names. And your language? It's a high-priest cult dialect from a fringe group."

"You've sort of lost me."

"All right, let me give you the nickel run down on the Sumerians. They were a branch of the Mesopotamians, but one that spoke what is now known as a 'language isolate'."

"Meaning there was no known preceding language," I interjected, excitement building.

"Precisely, yes. It has often been wondered just where – and how – in the world it originated. Among my peers, I'm a bit of a radical thinker. I'm considered an outsider. Hell, even a pariah, of a kind."

"You don't seem too distraught over that."

"I'm not! I know what I believe to be true, and I can't waver from that. I believe that there was a Chinese cult which found their way to Sumer, and were accepted as high priests. I further espouse the belief that cult practices were performed or held within the topmost portions of the Sumerian ziggurats.

"With all of that in mind, I believe that what you have here is evidence of my theory being partially true. Although, admittedly, this work comes far later than would support my suppositions."

"But what if you're right?" I asked. "What if there *was* a cult. And what if their language *was* a result of the interference of the Chinese."

"And what if it was a tradition that was carried on, in secret, until at least the time the book was written."

"It's a stretch."

"It's all of that," Ming concurred. "But it's the only thing I can come up with that makes sense." A pause, and then, "And there's one other thing."

"That being?"

"This isn't the first example of this writing that's come to light."

Now he had my full attention. "Indeed?"

"I made some calls to some friends in low places. Apparently, the Vatican has a copy of a similar work in their collection."

"You're joking."

"I'm not, no."

"I don't suppose that we could-"

"Probably not a chance in hell, no," he deflated.

"Well, then it doesn't matter," I sighed.

"It might not," he agreed. "If I didn't know someone who happened to have a copy."

"I thought the Vatican didn't permit-"

"They don't. And just don't ask questions. I'm going to pick it up tonight."

"Can I meet you afterward?"

"What, tonight?" Ming balked.

"Of course."

"I won't even have the thing until after midnight."

"I have nowhere to be."

"All right, how about this. I'll come to you. The last thing I need is to shit where I eat."

It took me a minute to size up the turn of phrase, but I got the gist. "All right. I'm in-"

"I know where you're at."

I blanched, and began to speak.

"Look, I needed to know who you were, and what you were all about. Turns out you're just a normal guy with an abnormal artifact."

"I could have told you that."

"I'm sure you could have. The problem was, I wouldn't have believed it."

12:48 am

The knock on the door was dainty, almost feminine. Looking through the peephole, I espied one Ming Ho. He looked a little worse for wear, tired, and skittish.

"Did you get it?" I asked, ushering him in.

"Yeah," he replied, furtively scanning the room. "I don't think anyone followed me."

"Seriously, Ming, you need to calm down. Who'd be following you?"

"The Swiss Guard, for starters."

"Why on Earth would they be here, looking for you?"

"They're tasked with guarding-"

"The Vatican. I know that. But why would they care?"

"Because I think you have something that might belong to them."

"Might belong to-"

"It's possible," he said, plopping on the room's tiny couch, making use of the coffee table before it, "that the book in your possession was once in the Vatican archives."

"It's stolen?" I wailed.

"I don't know," Ming said, opening his laptop.

I took a seat beside him.

"The fellow who got this for me mentioned that there were two volumes stored together. The scan, however, only showed one."

"So we can presume that if it *was* stolen, it was done before scanners existed. Or at the very least before it could get scanned."

"Right."

"Wasn't he curious about why you wanted this then?"

'Oh he was all of that. In fact," here, he hesitated, "I had to show him mine before he showed me his."

"You *what!*" I shrieked, face flushing.

"I didn't have a choice!" Ming fired back.

"Of course you did!"

"No, I didn't. He was asking questions. I was being honest with him, because that's how he rolls. His curiosity on the matter is more academic in nature than it is akin to your own."

"How do you know that for certain, though?"

"Because he's thirteen, and his parents wouldn't just let him gallivant around the world."

"Your contact is *thirteen*?"

"He's a hacker, and he's something far beyond precocious. The kid's a genius, and if he doesn't invent time travel, I'll be shocked. But he's still just a kid, too."

"How does a kid-"

"If I knew, I'd have hacked the Vatican myself. The point is, I don't. He does. He did. We needed him."

I sighed in assent. What was done was done. "Agreed."

"So," he said, perking up a bit, "it references the two volumes as a unit. They're cataloged in Italian as '*Libro Dei Nomi*'"

"'*The Book of Names*'," I responded.

"Got it in one. The first book is about forty pages in length."

"Same as this one."

"Yep. The scans are a bit crude by today's standards, but they're clear enough for me to see that they're more of the same writing. All forty pages are filled, for the most part. No illustrations."

"Any changes in handwriting?"

"Not a one, no."

This got me to thinking, as he tabbed through the Vatican's scanned pages. "Perhaps," I said at length, "the first book is a primer. The second book is the actionable work."

"That makes sense, but a primer for what?"

"I wish I knew."

♦   ♦   ♦   ♦   ♦

We spent the next few hours poring over the scans of the two works. I had ported a copy to my laptop, so we found ourselves tethered to the closest outlet, not speaking except to pose a new question for rumination.

The sun came up, and I began to get that ugly feeling that one gets after having not freshened up in a day, while also having been in one place, sweating, for far too long.

I needed a shower.

As the hot water cascaded over me, I drowsed. At one point, my head was leaned against the fiberglass surround and I could hear the thuds of morning ablutions, and muffled conversation from the adjacent room.

When I emerged, refreshed but no less tired, I found Ming as I had left him. He was focused on his laptop screen with an intensity that would make a laser blush the with shame of inadequacy.

"Aren't you tired?"

"I'm exhausted," Ming replied. "But how often do you get to look at something like these two works?"

He had a point, though I scarcely thought it meritorious of further scrutiny. The fact was that we were stuck. We had no further notion about anything contained in either volume that we had not had when we began poring over them.

I said as much.

"Well, just a second ago – now, don't get mad – I tried something."

"Why would I get mad?"

"I've been poking around the works with a hypothesis in mind. Inside of that structure, I think I teased out a few more clues."

"Why didn't you say something?" I hollered, returning to my still-warm place on the couch.

"Because it's sort of insane. I-"

At first I believed that Ming was pausing in an effort to construct his next sentence. When his eyes went wide, I knew something was wrong.

"Ming? Ming! What's wrong?" I asked, frightened. I grabbed his hand in a futile effort to gain understanding.

With his other hand, he pointed to his head. He wasn't breathing. He passed out.

I dialed 911, and began cardiopulmonary respiration. I kept pumping away in life-giving rhythm until the EMT's arrived.

We didn't need them, though. We needed the coroner.

♦   ♦   ♦   ♦   ♦

The police arrived soon after, followed by one Detective Jonas. My statement was taken. A few glances with implications of perversity were offered up by the police. I wasn't interested in rising to the indignity, so I remained silent on the matter, pragmatic and holding firm to my loose story. It was chock full of holes with regard to specifics. Still, like Swiss cheese, it remained passable in its own form.

I would later learn that Ming had passed away from an acute brain aneurysm. He was only twenty-one.

When the police had left, I sat back down on the sofa. I felt like a tiny sailboat in the heart of the doldrums. All around me was a sea of humanity, yet none of them could assist me in solving my problem. The books were so enigmatic that even the most respected scholars on the planet couldn't quantify their contents. Yet Ming had done what they could not. And before he had died, he had hinted at more.

As I looked before me, I saw my friend's volume laid open to the first fresh page. There, at the top and in faint pencil, was scrawled Ming's name. It was not in the polyalphabetic script of the book itself, but in plain old English.

I replayed Ming's final statements in my head. Over and over, until I had convinced myself that it could not be otherwise.

"That's impossible," I whispered.

But what if it wasn't?

◆   ◆   ◆   ◆   ◆

Over the ensuing days, I holed up in my hotel room. I checked in digitally with both my patron and the institutions of higher learning who were having a go at deciphering the work. So far, I had told no one of Ming's find, though I did mention his untimely passing.

Whether awake or drowsing, my mind kept coming back to a single notion. Ming had said that he had a hypothesis. It couldn't have been a correct one, if one were to presume that writing his name in the pages could have-

No. I can't believe it's possible.

Even so, my mind would not be silent in the matter.

I needed to test the theory. To prove once and for all that the asinine notions that refused to vacate my mind were nothing more than a fallacy. It was a whimsical concept brought about by too much time in professional contemplation of dark works of literature, coupled with an overactive imagination attempting to make sense of the seemingly nonsensical death of an intelligent young man with a great deal of promise.

The weather outside had turned overcast, as a pall of grey swept over the morning's blue sky. A pigeon was perched on my window ledge, shielded from the blowing wind's brunt by an outcropping of masonry.

"This is stupid," I said, as I stood and walked toward the nightstand. I opened the drawer and found my clutch. Within were a smattering of day-to-day necessities: paper, pen, calculator, business cards, a few spare bucks, and a mechanical pencil.

Tossing the clutch on the disheveled bedspread, I stalked defiantly back to the couch. Sitting, I grasped the book. I set it in my lap, ungloved, and stared at the faint letters of Ming's name. Then I looked toward the pigeon. Upon the page, just below his name, in the faintest of faint pencil, I wrote 'pigeon'.

I watched. I waited.

Nothing happened.

Then, as a smile rent my mouth, I watched in horror as the pigeon tumbled off the edge of the building. I had seen no hint that it was attempting to take flight. It just stiffened and rolled.

Flying from my seat, I stared out my window in the defiant hope that I would once more make it out, in flight and entirely fine.

I never saw it again.

Over the next day's time I did not sleep. Rather, I spent my days writing 'pigeon' upon the page each time one alighted on my room's sill. And as before, with each writing, the pigeon would go stiff and roll off the edge.

Five times in all.

Before a sixth potential victim could be tested, there was a knock at my room's door.

I hadn't ordered room service since the day prior, nor was I expecting anyone. Even so, my curiosity got the better of me and I found myself instinctively tiptoeing on the carpet toward the door. Looking out the peephole, my eyes met with a sight they did not expect. It was Professor Balkan.

Heaving a sigh, I unlocked the door and threw it wide. "Professor Balkan!" I said, more cordially than I felt.

"Indeed!" came the petite man's reply. "Might I come in?"

"Of course."

It was apparent that neither the room, nor its state, held any particular interest for Professor Balkan. As though he were the occupant, he strode over to the couch and made himself comfortable in the exact spot where Ming had perished. Surveying the contents of the impish coffee table before him, he stopped me dead in my tracks. "O-ho! You've found the second book!"

◆　　　◆　　　◆　　　◆　　　◆

"It's been a long time since I saw it," was his response to my blank look of surprise.

"It's in the Vatican collection," was all I managed, as I sat down next to him, wary but curious.

"Right where *this* one is supposed to be. I know! I put them there!"

"You...put them there?"

"Indeed!" He paused a beat, and then said, "Dear boy, won't you sit? You're making me nervous just hovering like that."

Mouth still half-agape, I did as bidden.

"You see," the Professor began, "I know full well what those books are. My father was in a platoon that was instrumental in raiding a Kunstschutz hoard. And before you ask, the Kunstschutz were Göring's units that were responsible for the false preservation of artifacts and antiquities in the guise of 'saving' them from destruction within invaded countries and territories.

"What it was, was wholesale theft and plunder on a grand scale. Plain and simple. Still, the Nazis didn't like to call a spade a spade, and found grandiose and flowery ways to refer to the most heinous things. I imagine Hitler didn't fart, but instead 'organically enriched the air'."

This last statement made me laugh. The whole situation I now found myself in was ludicrous, but the withered man's tale seemed credible. At least, it seemed to him to be.

"One of the things my father's group repatriated, as it were," Professor Balkan continued, "was a large collection of rare books and manuscripts. I don't know what ever became of the remainder of them, but my Father somehow absconded with a pair of leftovers. Those are the books you see before you. One in digital form, and one in physical form."

So many questions were aflutter in my mind. It was a chaos of inquisition that very nearly got the better of my tongue. Even so, I began my inevitable inquiry with, "Why did you pretend not to know what the book was?"

"If you knew what these books were, you'd have done the same. You see, I spent years poring over these books. My father lost interest in them almost as soon as they had arrived. But to a young boy they were a strange and wonderful thing just beckoning to be understood. We didn't have the Internet back then. Hell, my family didn't even have a television. We had radio, and books, and people to entertain us. I'll tell you this – we were much better off than your connected society of today.

"Still, no sense in pining for the past in a future made whole, eh?

"Suffice it to say that I spent years writing letters to scholars, requesting books at my library, and mail ordering every book on the occult I could afford from the periodic catalogs that I received. My mother thought it unwholesome, while my father considered it nothing more than a child's mind growing and learning on its own, driven by an insatiable curiosity.

"They were both right.

"One day, I received a letter from a fellow named John Rupert Firth at *The School of African and Oriental Studies*. He was most excited, you see, because his mind had wrapped around the same premise that your young Mr. Ho had.

"You mean has," I feinted.

"I mean *had*. When I heard of his demise, I feared the worst and came here straight away."

So there it was.

"You're expecting me to believe that the book had something to do with his death?"

"I'm guessing that it's a certainty," he pronounced. Then, a new volley of fire, "Tell me, have you tested it yourself?"

The stern and paternal gaze that he leveled at me dared me to lie. In the end, I chose the truth. "I have, yes. It took me a while to puzzle out how to do it, but then I settled on pigeons."

"Most ingenious! Cruel, but ingenious. And did it work?"

I sighed, acquiescing to the truth of the matter, "It did. Yes. Repeatedly."

"I thought as much," he said, nodding somberly. "Thank God you didn't get a wild hair and try it on your fellow man. I know the draw is strong. Once I realized what the book said, I did nothing but think about using it, night and day. It invaded my dreams, and tormented my waking hours."

"The compulsion was there," I admitted. "But I don't think that I could ever kill anyone. Even with a book. Never underestimate what you're capable of. Instead, remain stalwart in the hope that you'll never have dire need to learn."

"So what do we do with the book now? I'm bound by my friend to gather intelligence on it, to learn its meaning, its content, and its origin."

This statement resulted in a look of utter confusion on the part of the Professor. "My dear boy, what we *do* with it is return it to the Vatican archives posthaste. Can't you see what's happened here? This book has become a physical force upon the world around it. Even in what should have been one of the safest prisons in the world, it would still not be bound. It found a way out."

"Do you realize how ridiculous you sound right now?" I scoffed.

"I'm telling you, the thing is evil. The power within those pages is an umbilicus to something humanity is better rid of. Somewhere along the line, most of us recognized this. The authors of this work either didn't, or chose not to. Either way, they left behind this legacy of darkness to besmirch society's future.

"I've tried to destroy it hundreds of times. But I can't. It won't permit itself to be destroyed."

"You say it's evil," I replied, "yet you haven't told me what it *does*."

This brought the Professor up short. It was evident that he was weighing his next statement with great care. Finally, he spoke, "What it does, dear boy, is rob Peter to pay Paul. The names written within are the names of people. Living, breathing, people. At least they were. Once their names are written into the pages, they cannot be unwritten. Their life force is transferred to the scribe who imparted the name.

"The problem comes with overuse. Over time, the amount of life force imparted becomes less and less. To the point where the writer must write more names, more often."

I sat in stunned silence for a moment. Then, I asked, "So whomever was writing these names-"

"Was an evil git who probably lived a good long time on someone else's nickel. Yes."

Dear Lord, I thought. *How could someone do that?*

I felt my pencil in my hand. I didn't even remember having picked it up. The Professor reached for the book. I was faster. His look of confusion turned to a dawning realization of fear. Before I realized what I had done, I had written in the book, just below the word pigeon.

Professor Balkan

It less than twenty seconds, he was gone. Just as Ming had been.

And so, dear reader, it went on. For years I lived. Then decades. I watched as the world around me found new and more unique ways of destroying itself.

I watched as war was regulated, while business was deregulated. Both were destructive, but at least one was focused. The Earth had a difficult time supporting the populous that was mortally wounding her.

At first, I only used the book to offer salvation to terminal patients in great pain. Then, I would use it on the occasional dictator, or person whom I felt was of no meritorious use to their fellow man. Then it was simple bullies. People I disliked.

One day dawned, and I knew what I had to do. I saw the world dying around me, and so I felt obliged to take action. I had no regrets when I wrote my final entry.

All of humanity.

I don't know how long ago that was. I don't mark time anymore. I've learned that I can be injured. I learned this the hard way, when I broke my arm a few years after I killed the Professor. My assumption is that I am still mortal when it comes to my physical form. So I take great care to keep my body protected.

Even as I write this, however, I look back upon my foolishness. I am all but certain that I am dying before my time. I have an infection in my foot, caused by a deep gash I received days ago. My veins are dark, and my leg is swollen beyond belief. Stinky pus runs freely from the wound, and the pain is agonizing. I have done all I can to treat myself, but I am now unable to move.

On the horizon, the sun is beginning to set. It's the sort of thing that happens every day, yet most of us fail to take notice of, let alone appreciate for the splendor and grandeur it offers up, asking nothing in return.

I hope that someone, someday, finds this. I hope that it is understood. I hope that humanity, or the next iteration like it, learn to understand the failings of the past, in an effort to make a better future.

I stop writing, and place the final logbook in amongst all the others. I close the stainless steel box. It was originally designed for fishermen, but I considered it my best hope of preservation of the logs I will leave behind.

Once the container is sealed, I pick up the book. There is still room to write in the pages. In it, I write two final things:

Anyone who attempts to use this book.

Me.

177

ROCKFORD'S ROLE IN THE CRIME OF THE CENTURY

TIM HUGHES

It was the heyday of yellow journalism, and the Hearst press wasted no time declaring it "The Crime of the Century". Obviously, it wasn't. A decade later, the Lindbergh kidnapping was labeled "The Crime of the Century", followed a decade after that by the real Crime of the Century, the Nazi genocide of the Jewish people. Nonetheless, the events occurring on a May afternoon in Chicago ninety-one years ago, still hold a fascination and have spawned plays, novels, movies (one an Alfred Hitchcock film titled *Rope*), various memoirs, documentaries, and even a musical!

Two Chicago youth, college graduates still in their teens (one was the youngest ever to graduate from the University of Michigan), both the sons of millionaires (the father of one was vice president of Sears & Roebuck, and a personal friend of Chicago's mayor), kidnapped and murdered a fourteen-year-old cousin of one of the killers, a child of wealth, like themselves, and sought to collect a ransom in an effort to commit what they deemed the "perfect crime", and to experience the thrill of killing someone. The accidental dropping of a pair of eyeglasses by one of the killers at the crime scene led to a diligent clerk's tracing the glasses in the optometrist's office where she worked. This act quickly led to the killers' arrest, trial, and conviction. They were sentenced to prison terms of life plus ninety-nine years.

The crime was so bizarre, so shocking for its callousness and brutality, and so unlike what one would expect in criminals capable of such a deed, it became an international sensation. The events of the murder, the detection of the suspects, and the subsequent trial, in which the killers were defended by renowned attorney Clarence Darrow, gained a worldwide audience.

I first learned of the Loeb/Leopold Crime of the Century while reading Meyer Levin's bestselling novel *Compulsion* (based on the murder and made into a movie starring Orson Welles, and Dean Stockwell as one of the killers). In the film's closing scene, the famous eyeglasses that led to the killers were super imposed on the screen.

My mother worked as a file clerk for the Smith Oil Company in northwest Rockford. On certain Saturdays, she would go to the office to catch up on work. I would go with her to sit and read. The novel I was reading that particular day was *Compulsion*. My mother objected to my reading it, claiming that I couldn't understand what it was about. On the narrative level it was easy to understand with

181

its vivid imagery. She was right, however, for on another level I didn't understand the obliquely worded passages dealing with Leopold and Loeb's intimate relationship. We were overheard discussing my mother's objections by a coworker who had also come in to catch up on work. She turned in her chair and casually asked me, "What do you want to know about Leopold and Loeb? I'm the one who traced Leopold's glasses."

Her name was Leona Reimer. She was treasurer of the Smith Oil Company for a number of years. Leona was a heavyset, middle-aged woman who was highly regarded by Smith Oil employees. She went on to tell me that her supervisor at Chicago's Almer Coe Optical Company, where she had worked at the time, was concerned for her safety after she traced the glasses. In the aftermath, he sent her away from Chicago.

In the years that followed her revelation, I never thought to ask my mother if Miss Reimer had ever again mentioned the tracing of the glasses, which became crucial to solving the case. I did ask my mother's sister, who also knew Leona, if she had ever heard the woman speak of it. She said that, no, Leona had never mentioned the case to her. She went on to add that Reimer's reputation for truthfulness was beyond question, and that she would never have lied about anything, and especially something like that.

All I've been able to learn about the actual tracing of the glasses is that the Almer Coe Company put its clerks to work on the task. The glasses were a common prescription, but the one found at the murder site had special frames. These frames were manufactured elsewhere, and sold only by that Chicago optical firm, and just three times. One purchaser, thirty years later, became the judge who denied Julius and Ethel Rosenberg a final stay of execution. Reimer may have been the clerk that made the actual discovery. There is only one fact I'm aware of supporting her claim of having made that all important discovery. She was born in Rockford on July 8, 1900 and died here on December 2, 1965 and is buried in the Masonic Circle in Willwood Burial Park. She lived in Rockford all her life except for one year, the year 1924—the year of the Crime of the Century.

Reimer's connection may be the only direct Rockford link to the crime, but there are other associations as well. Jacob Franks, father of the murder victim, once owned the famous Rockford Watch Company. Anna Loeb, the mother of Richard Loeb, one of the killers, had a close association with Jane Addams and Hull House. My great grandfather, George Mundy, a Rockford realtor, had business dealings with one of Loeb's uncles.

My grandfather was foreman of the Smith Oil Company refinery that adjoined the company's office building. He was an unsophisticated, plain-spoken man who dropped out of school in 1910 at age twelve. He was a young parent at the time of the Loeb/Leopold case, and always held the opinion that the two killers should be hanged – by their testicles.

As I said, my grandfather was a plain spoken, blunt man.

My mother and I lived with my grandparents, and one night, in 1958, we were discussing Leopold's impending parole (Loeb having been murdered by a prison inmate in 1936), and I mentioned in passing the name of Clarence Darrow, who had been their defense attorney.

"Oh, that sonofabitch," my grandfather grumbled. "I had a run in with him on the loading dock at Smith Oil."

I looked at my grandfather in disbelief. Clarence Darrow, the greatest trial lawyer of his time, on the loading dock at Smith Oil Company on Kilburn Avenue in Rockford? Impossible. Grandpa must have it wrong.

"No," he added when I questioned him further. "He was trying to organize a labor union at the plant. I told him to get the hell out of there."

I let it go at that. I couldn't imagine the most famous trial lawyer of his day on Kilburn Avenue in Rockford. It made no sense.

Twenty years later, while browsing in a used book store, I came across a paperback edition of Darrow's famous twelve hour summation in the Loeb/Leopold case. When I went to purchase it, the store's proprietor noticed on the book's cover that the two cities where it had been published were San Francisco and Rockford. Why Rockford, he wondered? Why not New York or Chicago? I, too, puzzled for a time over why it would have been published here, and not somewhere else more logical and urban. After briefly considering it, I went on to more important things. Some fifteen years later, while researching a different subject, I came across the name of Faye Lewis. At that point I realized that perhaps Darrow *had* at one time or another been on the loading dock of Smith Oil.

Faye Lewis, like Clarence Darrow, was an American original. He opened a tobacco store at 314 West State Street in downtown Rockford in 1875 and turned it into a highly successful enterprise with outlets in Milwaukee and Eau Claire, Wisconsin. An advocate of prison reform and a passionate opponent of the death penalty, he hired mostly former convicts to work in his cigar manufactory. In 1903 he published a book denouncing the Winnebago County Jail, comparing it to the infamous "Black Hole of Calcutta". Firmly convinced that toy soldiers turned boys into blood thirsty soldiers later in life, he journeyed along with a Jewish rabbi to Nuremberg, Germany, then the world capitol of toy soldier manufacturing, and campaigned for the owners of those businesses to cease making toy soldiers. He also served as the supervisor of Winnebago County Animal Services, and was elected president of the Rockford Park District in 1937. His home at 704 N. Church Street, now owned by Meld, became a gathering place for artists and intellectuals. Among his visitors was the poet Edgar Lee Masters, who wrote a poem about Lewis that appeared in Masters' sequel to *Spoon River Anthology.*

The earliest newspaper account I have of Darrow being in Rockford is 1889 to give a speech, and it's most likely the two met at one of Henry George's Single Tax Club meetings. Lewis called Darrow "My friend for life" and kept a bust of him until his own death in February 1949.

Most Darrow biographers pay scant attention to Lewis. John A. Farrell, author of the recent Darrow biography - considered to be the most definitive work yet on Darrow's life - mentions Lewis only twice in his five hundred page biography, and that in passing. I believe the relationship between the two is yet to be fully explored concerning the man Lewis called "My friend for life."

Then there was Alice Beal Parson. She was the granddaughter of a popular Rockford mayor, niece of the founder of the Mendelsohn Club, a graduate of Rockford Female Seminary (now Rockford University), who married into a prominent Rockford family and lived in an exclusive Rockford neighborhood on Spring Creek Road. She would have been destined to become a leading city socialite except for one thing. She was widely known and bitterly hated as the "Red Queen of Seventh Street", for immigrant workers' parades she led through downtown Rockford, and found herself on the wrong side of a door being broken down by Federal agents as the infamous

Palmer Raids swept across the nation in January 1920. As she was led to a waiting police wagon, she spotted a reporter for the Rockford Morning Star covering the raid and shouted to him, "Tell the world I'm a member of the Communist Labor Party!"

Darrow defended Parson and fellow communists in a trial in the Winnebago County Courthouse in April that year and won an acquittal for the defendants. Soon after, Parson's husband divorced her and she moved to New York City. It was there that she eventually wrote a novel about Rockford, and her sedition trial, that became the first work of fiction published by publishing giant Funk and Wagnalls. In the novel, Darrow appears as himself.

Leopold was paroled from prison in March, 1958 after serving thirty-four years of his life plus ninety-nine year sentence. Ironically, the day of his release was the twentieth anniversary of Clarence Darrow's death. There is a famous Life magazine photo of his throwing up on the side of the interstate highway, leading into Chicago, due to his being unused to the speed of a modern automobile. The driver of the car, Ralph Newman, an antiquarian Chicago book dealer, would himself gain notoriety by becoming the last person indicted in the Watergate scandal, this for back dating Nixon's vice presidential papers for tax purposes.

Following his parole, Leopold lived in a remote Puerto Rican village where he worked in the local hospital as an x-ray technician and was known as "Mr. Lollipops" for the lollipops he always carried in his pocket for children in the hospital. In 1961 he married a Baltimore widow who ran a florist shop in San Juan.

After receiving permission from his attorney, I corresponded briefly with Leopold shortly before his death of a heart attack at age 65. In my letter I asked him what his impression had been of Carl Sandburg's testimony on his behalf before the parole board. In his reply, Leopold complimented me for contacting his lawyer for permission to correspond with him. Such courtesy was rare these days, Leopold told me in the letter that he wrote back. He then answered my question, stating that Sandburg took the parole board by storm in the way General Grant had taken Richmond during the Civil War. That was the extent of our correspondence. When he died on August 29, 1971, Chicago newspapers carried a headline that read: The Death and Life of Nathan Leopold.

The Loeb/Leopold case, in a peculiar way, has become "The Crime of the Century". The term 'Loeb/Leopold Syndrome' has

185

joined the lexicon of criminology definitions to indicate those who, by themselves, would never commit a serious crime, but would do so in tandem with another.

Having taught for some thirty years in public schools, I often found myself dealing with troubled youth from broken homes and bad environments. In spite of such factors, they knew where not to cross the line. As such, I am less favorably inclined toward Leopold than in my adolescence, when I was influenced by the somewhat sympathetic portrayal of him in *Compulsion*. I think that, had he and Loeb been executed, it would have at least brought what we now call closure to the victim's family. No earthly power can parole fourteen year old Bobby Franks from the sentence Loeb and Leopold imposed on him. I believe their crime was motivated in large part by a gratuitous sense of entitlement, due to their own background as sons of privilege. That they robbed another son of privilege from the right to live out his life is truly sad.

OCTANE GIRL

JASON LEVISKAS

Editor's note: In an effort to preserve the author's original concept, this work has been gapped between stanzas due to space constraints in width.

188

Once upon a cold afternoon I stumbled on a work day into a different coffee shop;

The coffee was ordered warm and made from their highest Octane.

I could see the coffee pour and with the delivery to the table my jaw slightly a drop;

There the Octane Girl I first saw, beautiful from afar needing no eyestrain.

Her dark curly hair and glasses are always a welcoming sight;

Her face is always greeting people with a friendly glare.

Her blue eyes glimmer at you like the stars on a clear night;

Octane Girl's beauty is timeless and true...that makes her very rare.

She is beautiful yes, but is she also nice too;

She keeps pouring coffee and has a way to keep me talking.

She is a good chatter too and it makes the coffee and I brew;

I think Octane Girl is nice, but people can fake nice there is more to her that's foretelling.

Sometimes a woman can be sweet and it not be true;

A good woman in this world can be hard to find.

The more we talk and share, she reveals without knowing her virtue;

Octane Girl is more than a pretty face, and a nice girl, she has a genuine good heart that is kind.

Knowing what I know has been an accidental discovery about another;

The knowledge that has been learned presents the question of what a shy guy is supposed to do.

Even though confidence has been gained, the pursuit and approach has begun to a stir;

Octane Girl is worth fighting 100 men for, line them up I say, but then why can't I get the right words out for her to stew?

This poem she will surely read...

I hope she will laugh and smile but this poem still might not make it clear;

Octane Girl at the very least should know my respect for her and that my goal one day is to share a beer.

DESERT GODDESS

TERRY STOLZ

Eyes of copper
Heart of gold
You lust for water
So life's seeds can grow
Forget your dolor
Your barren rock
Your golden sand

For there sprouts a city
In your vast wasteland
Infested with gutter-scum and whores
Where sin is fed to their young and old.
Oh Desert Goddess
Return this town to the dust it was
For towns like this
Need grow no more
Let them cease to be
Wipe our memories clean
You are all that we need to see

Desert Goddess
You wear the sun as your shining crown
Golden sand
You wear for your flowing gown
You haven't the meadows, or flowers, or trees
But you have the enduring peace
A serenity unattainable by Man's greed

194

CORPORATIONS ARE PEOPLE TOO

HEATH D. ALBERTS

My phone buzzed. I stabbed the intercom button in retaliation.
"Yo!" I said.

"We need to talk."

It was Leroy. He was my boss, and also a royal pain in my ass
when it came to permitting me the unbridled latitude that I felt my
thirty-plus years as a print journalist should command.

"About?" I replied, passively defiant.

"My office," he replied. "Now."

I didn't like the sound of that, as he clicked off without further
utterance. I had known Leroy long enough to grudgingly respect his
opinions, while also having the uncanny knack of divining his
moods. His final sentence fell well outside of my existing framework
of knowledge on both of those fronts.

When I opened the door to his office, I made sure a jovial grin
was on my face. As though to say, 'It's all friendly on my end,
whatever you're about to chew me out for'.

"Sit," was his deadpan response.

I did as bid, attempting in vain to parse out the visage upon the
man before me. He sat behind his desk, clearly uncomfortable in his
chair. A chair that had been once been fashionable, had then fallen
well out of fashion, had become a physical joke, and yet had come
full circle as retro-hip. His normally healthy pallor was ashen. He just
looked worn out. Like a hole-riddled sock, he too was threadbare.

"I got a call from *Jovian*'s legal team about an hour ago."

"Oh, Jesus – *this* again!"

"Just listen," he commanded. He did so in a temperate voice. Had
he yelled, I would have been far less disconcerted.

"Fine."

"They're pursuing new action on the water rights story."

"They've been up our ass on that one since the story's ink hit the
paper," I retorted. "What else is new?"

"What's new," he said, still maintaining that horrible, even tone,
"is that they've done some research. Since the *Citizens United*
ruling, the expansion of corporate rights has been slowly accreting.
Durkin v. Intevac, Inc., as you've so often pointed out, was the
disputed ground zero for such things."

"You're not telling me anything that I don't know, Leroy. Now
please, just tell me why I'm in here."

"The board has met with regard to *Jovian*'s assertions. They've
spoken with ownership, and they all feel that we have been left

with no recourse but to terminate your employment immediately."

"What?" I couldn't have heard that right. That would not only be reactionary, but stupid as well. I was an above the fold section producer, and a front page regular as icing on that particular cake.

"I'm sorry. With the legislation that passed last month, *Jovian* has decided that they want to be the first to push the envelope of the legal boundaries of the verbiage. And apparently they've chosen us – chosen you – to do so with."

No, no, no, no, no, I thought. This is stupid. My career doesn't end like this. It *can't* end like this. As much as I wished it to be a sick joke, no one was laughing. I could see that Leroy's having been selected to be the bearer of the news was weighing heavily on him. Still, I couldn't sympathize. I was a healthy cash cow who was being sacrificed on an altar. An altar belonging to a God that no one in the public was worshipping.

"Leroy – and I say this with all due respect, here – this is bullshit."

Leroy blew out his cheeks, sighed, leaned back, and tented his fingers before him. His chair squeaked with a combination of age and lack of lubricant. "I know. I won't even pretend to argue with you. But the fact of the matter is that the accusations that you leveled in your piece are clearly making them uncomfortable."

"They *should* make them uncomfortable! They're raping the God-damned water system! A system, by the way, that rightfully belongs to the populous. And then they're charging them to buy back what was theirs to begin with. Not to mention something that's been a fundamental human right for as long as anyone can remember."

"The new laws permit grey areas, and those grey areas are being tested by corporations like *Jovian*. In this case, they're asserting that your piece is not only hearsay, it's also defamatory and damaging to their corporate image."

"Are you listening to yourself? You know as well as I do-"

"You're right," Leroy interrupted, "I do."

I backed down. Of course he did. Taking out my frustration on this poor sucker, who had been forced to impart this news, was tantamount to beating a baby for soiling its diaper. It was what a baby was expected to do. This, sadly, was a facet of what Leroy was expected to do in his position with the paper.

"I'm sorry," I said, deflating. I brought my demeanor back down to a conversational level. "Look, they can be angry. They can dislike the story. They can even openly contest it. But the facts are the facts. What I printed was based on credible sources, empirical data, and research. Period."

"I don't doubt that. Nor does the board, if I had to guess."

"Then what's the problem, here? Why the pressure to dismiss me? And moreover, why concede to it?"

"Over the past months, they've been quashing everyone and anyone who has spoken out about their water claims and practices. This time, our legal department feels that their claim – while grey in nature – has a chance at sticking."

"But it *shouldn't*!"

"'*Shouldn't*' isn't a factor. '*Can*' or '*cannot*' is. Their stance is that you've done them harm. And now they're preparing to demand their pound of flesh."

"But they'll never win a case like that!"

"Well, that's where things get hairy."

"Leroy, what aren't you telling me here?"

"They intend to bring suit against you, personally, in the French court of law. Their position is that *Citizens United* permitted corporations to function as people and, therefore, since they were wronged, they wish to take the matter up in a court of law. Because they're headquartered in France, but operate within the US as well, they feel that it is within their legal rights to assert wrongdoing and harm in the French judicial system, based on American law."

"That's preposterous!"

"It's happening," Leroy lamented. "And we've been advised that if we don't terminate your employment with the paper immediately that we will also be named as defendants in the upcoming suits."

"I can't believe this is happening," I said, empty. I should be distraught, but I was too numb and shocked to be. I felt like a piece of driftwood bobbing in the ocean. Barely afloat, and ever so inconsequential to my surroundings.

"You'll need a good lawyer," Leroy advised, taking an avuncular tone. "Word is that they plan to bury you in a deep legal crossfire. Even if they don't win, they intend to make an example of you."

"I'll be dead before all that's over, if they're really that set on doing such a ridiculous thing."

"Word is that they are," Leroy confided.

I could tell he wanted to say more, but it would only serve to parrot what I was already thinking. Everything in my life now belonged to them. They would ruin me, bankrupt me, and blackball me. I would die a pauper, a victim of their abyssal corporate coffers and their desire to have me as a guinea pig. A proving ground for future lambs to be led to new and differing slaughters.

Thirty years of building a life, gone. All because of a story founded in truth and principal.

A knock at the door behind me broke my reverie. I heard the door open, but I did not turn. I knew who it was.

"Demetrius," Leroy sighed, "please escort-"

"I'm going," I said, attempting to maintain what little dignity I had remaining. "I know my way."

CITY MARKET

TIM HUGHES

Editor's note: In an effort to preserve the author's original stanzas, this work's font size has been reduced to accommodate.

Rows of olive green buckets blazing with bundled sheaves of cut flowers,
rags of fire tossing across a grill where simmers the aroma of pizza;
its crisp, breaded smell tightening the mellow air and sending an alluring fragrance
drifting above a skyline cross stitched in blue and white tent tops
their breezy hues daubing the tree shaded marketplace
like strokes from a painter's brush,
while all around shoppers leisurely peruse
fruit and vegetable stands brimming with a reddish sheen of apples;
golden rows of rumpled skin oranges; boxes piled
with the purple glow of blueberries pyramiding into an overflow
side by side with scarlet blushing raspberries
and the smooth gleam of ripened tomatoes.

HEART OF OAK

HEATH D. ALBERTS

206

I don't remember anything about my formative weeks. I'd like to say that I do, but there's no point in pining for something that will simply never be. My pre-emergence youth will forever remain a personal mystery.

The first thing that I *do* recall is the sun. It was a breezy spring afternoon. There was a moment when I recognized myself, as myself, thereby becoming self-aware. All around me were my brothers and sisters, thousands of them residing in the canopy of robust foliage which served as our nurturing womb and nursery.

207

As the warmth of the leaf-dappled sun shone upon my green shell, I relished in its embrace. I felt the throb of life pulsing through me, even as the nesting robins occluded its rays from time to time. In that singular moment, I knew that I was something special. Something complex and beautiful, with the promise and capacity to become so much more. I did not know it then, but the odds of my doing so were staggeringly small.

I felt both a sadness and a relief that, unlike my red oak cousins, I would not have to wait for a full rotation of seasons to begin my journey. In the autumn, having survived the onslaught of wind, hail, birds, insects, and wildlife, I fell to the Earth.

The detachment was near to being free of anxiety. I would miss my family, and my parent, but I also craved a life of my own.

It was only a matter of days thereafter that the squirrels arrived in earnest. Along with their forest cousins, their mission was to pilfer as many of us from our second home as was possible before the winter set in. Unlike many of their cousins, they did not always eat us. I was one of the fortunate ones, in that regard. My squirrel, a female with an odd tail that had clearly been injured at one time, chose to remove me from the grove. Across a wide expanse of prairie grass, she placed me in the other side of the valley. There, conifers grew in significant numbers. I was, therefore, concerned that she might choose to deposit me there.

It was much to my relief when she began to furiously dig out a pocket of earth some distance from the foreign tree line. All the while, her sharp teeth dug into my shell, my cap having been lost somewhere in the bounding jaunt from my tree to this place. I had not even noticed when it had fallen off. Such was my sense of wonder at the journey upon which this defiant creature had taken me. With its loss, I felt both naked and liberated. Her malodorous breath swirled around me, coming in stronger puffs as she dug.

When she stopped, she dropped me without any sort of ceremony into the fresh hole, whereupon she proceeded to cover me with the loose earth. It was damp, and cold, and dark.

Despair immediately overcame me.

What do I do now?

How do I fulfill my purpose?

Will I ever feel the warmth of the sun upon me again?

I remained sentient for as long as I was able, until a powerful drowsiness overtook me. When I could no longer struggle against it, I embraced it. My fate was now in the hands of nature. There was nothing more that I could do, save wait and hope.

Moments later, I awoke with a start. At least I thought that it was moments later. As I took stock of myself, however, I realized that this simply could not be so. My shell was open to the world, and a stem and root had made significant inroads into forming.

When I once more felt the kiss of the sun, I was heartened as I had never been before.

I was alive!

I had weathered the irresistible slumber and emerged as something wholly new. My tiny sprout had scarcely broken the surface, but it was enough to reinvigorate me. I placed all of my energy into becoming.

As the days passed, my tiny root developed tendril hairs. My sprout pierced the empty air, climbing ever higher with each passing sunset. What might pass for leaves soon formed, and my stalk became semi-woody.

Through all of this, I recognized just how fortunate I was. I considered all of my brothers and sisters, and comprehended that there was no conceivable way that many of them had beaten the odds, as I had. Even so, I selfishly turned to pleading with the universe to permit me to grow, to flourish, to bear offspring of my own. To accomplish this meant not only surviving the elements, the fauna, and disease. It also meant doing so for twenty seasons.

This was no small feat. I was mournful when comprehending the enormity of the proposition.

Still, I had hope.

I bore nothing that I was proud to call true foliage that year, before a dormancy overtook me. When I awoke the following spring, I found that a new spurt of energy had overtaken me. My taproot had begun to define itself. I even bore a few respectable leaves. I still recall the first time that the breeze caught them in full, playing them about in the air as the wind made its own way around them. It was a cathartic sensation, and one I shall never forget for all of my years.

In my fifteenth season, I was struck by lightning. It was an excruciating experience, though one I managed to survive. Even so, I would bear the damage of the incident for the remainder of my days. My body had twisted and contorted with violence as the moisture within me turned from symbiotic friend into destructive foe. Some of my limbs were obliterated entirely. One limb broke at a high joint, leaving an open wound that simply begged for infection or infestation – or both. The worst part, though, was the twist that it put into the upper part of my trunk. It was a twist that I would struggle to right, but one that would never permit me to appear the same again.

Even so, I was alive. And that was everything.

In my twenty-first season, I felt a change come over me. I had reached sexual maturity. It wasn't a progression so much as a near-instantaneous surety. When the first tinges of another tree's pollen, as well as my own, made their way onto my stigma I was overjoyed. I was humbled that I had been provided such a beautiful opportunity. I made the best of it, encouraging my vascular system to work their hardest to feed and nurture me and, therefore, my offspring.

As they developed, my thoughts turned to darker things.

How many of these magnificent acorns would not be afforded the same mystical opportunity that I had been?

How many would end up mislaid, eaten, or barren?

It was a concept too dire to contemplate. Instead, I chose to focus on the positives. Some of these acorns *would* make it, just as I had. They would be my silent legacy upon the world when I was no more. This brought a joy to me that bordered on abreaction. I would become a chain in a link of oaken lineage. It was an honor I would bear proudly, with my canopy lofted high.

That fall, I was a parent. The upwelling of chaotic emotion was profound and sublime. I mattered. For years thereafter, I brought more beautiful offspring into the world.

It was during my twenty-eighth season that something changed. I had seen people before, though seldom. At first, they were but tiny motes of notable movement upon the distant landscape. The

209

second year there were more still. The third year they brought with them machines. I watched in horror as they obliterated an entire grove of maples. These had grown upon a nearby hillock, and had been there for as long as I had existed. In only a few days, the entire stand had been uprooted, sawn, and burned. What remained was nothing but an amalgam of soil and plant detritus. All of the animals that often frequented the grove were scattered, or seen no more.

How could they do that?

How could they take something which had taken so long to create and develop, and wipe if from the face of the planet in such a short time?

I would not find out why until the following spring when still more machines were brought in. They were accompanied by a hive of activity as a stretch of flat black ribbon was laid across the denuded landscape. Even the hills and valleys were not immune to the interference of man. They were moved, modified, or eliminated altogether in an effort to satisfy the passage of the inert blackness. It was a defilement that was too heinous to comprehend, yet one which I failingly struggled to ignore.

When I went dormant that fall, I felt a fear that I had not felt in any of my thirty-one seasons. For the first time since I had fallen, I feared for my very existence.

The following season I awoke to a more peaceful and serene surrounding. Gone were the chaos of men in strange garb. In their place were a few random smatterings of workers, though they were seldom seen in groups, or for very long.

Before I went dormant that season, yellow stripes were added to the black ribbon. This, I felt, added a bit of much needed cheeriness, though did little to enamor me, nor endear me to it. It was an ugly blight upon a peaceful landscape. It did not belong. Yet men had placed it there, just the same. Its dominance was imposed upon all of the living things in the little valley.

For seasons thereafter, there were constant streams of things moving to and fro upon the black ribbon, carrying people within. Day and night, they moved back and forth, back and forth. I perceived early on that most were unique. This made me wonder at length where they were going, and what manner of things they were.

Perhaps, I once considered, *they are like acorns, too.*

It was during my seventieth season that I felt something amiss in my lower regions. I had served as a home for birds on more occasions than I could recall. This, however, was a new feeling of movement. It would take me a further eight seasons to comprehend what was occurring beneath and inside me.

The culprits were ants. Big, black, ants. They spent their days toiling, moving every which way until I could often not tell where one began and the next ended. Still, I realized that they were delving deeper and deeper into me. At first, I didn't mind giving a part of myself to feed something else. When the realization dawned that they were not eating of me, but only living within me, I was angered. It was one thing to share oneself for the greater good of the whole. It was quite another to waste that sacrifice wantonly.

Over the ensuing few seasons I made peace with their presence. Their colony grew, and I almost enjoyed their company. Even if I wasn't sustaining them bodily, I was still sustaining them against the elements, and permitting them to create new life. This became enough to satisfy me.

It was in my eighty-seventh year when I began to feel frailer. My awakening in the spring was more laborious and sluggish than it had ever been. My outlook was further soured when I took stock of my trunk. The ants had experienced exponential growth, and with it came further ingress throughout my body. They had gone from nuisance to destroyer. If they continued their single-minded drive into my trunk, they would soon encounter more and more vital components, while further weakening me.

On a cold and rainy spring day, I lost all concern about the ants. This was the day that the men came back. As before, they came in loose groups at first, their conveyances bounding over the uneven land in an ungainly and unnatural manner. The closer they crept, the more alarmed I became.

Across the field, and on a mild slope, grew one of my offspring. I had watched the squirrel snatch its acorn and bound away with it, decades ago. With each passing season, whenever this happened, it would give me a start as I plead for mercy that my acorns would find fertile ground, and not the stomach of a hungry squirrel. Most times I would never come to know their specific fates. Sometimes, I would watch my offspring devoured right beneath my canopy. It was a rending experience, but I came to accept it as yet another component of the symbiotic nature of life.

As the men neared my offspring, I felt a tension within my fibers. Instead, their conveyance passed it and continued onward. At this point I would normally have eased my tensions. This would have been the case, were they not now coming straight toward me.

They stopped their conveyance in close proximity to where I was rooted. As they exited the confines, they headed to the rear. Here, they each grasped a metal cylinder. The top portions were the same hue as the skins I had seen men wear before, and also matched some of the fall foliage that I would witness each year in the valley.

The cylinders were opened by the men, and they proceeded into the neighboring stand of conifers. Here, they began spraying large dots of color upon the bark of dozens of firs. They continued in this manner for quite some time, with each passing moment moving closer and closer to me. It was late morning when one of the men stood beneath my canopy.

"How about this one, Merle?"

"What, the oak?"

"Yeah."

"I think it'll be okay."

The man beneath me shrugged, and began to walk away. The other man seemed to contemplate something, looking for a long moment at the ribbon of black.

Before the man beneath me had left my canopy's shade, the other fellow hollered anew. "You know what? Yeah, better tag that one, too."

The second man just gave a grunt, turned, and approached me. I felt the odd sensation of something entirely foreign coating a portion of my bark. It was acrid and strange and altogether unpleasant.

An hour later, they were gone.

A full phase-cycle of the moon had nearly passed before more men arrived in the valley. With them came the same large conveyances that I had seen before. My dread was entire. I watched in horror as they proceeded their onslaught against the color-spotted conifers. Their machines ripped through decades of growth in seconds, annihilating everything they touched.

I felt panic. It was a genuine dread the likes of which I had never experienced. Somehow I knew what was coming. I deluded myself for the first two days. I stopped when I was the final tree standing.

"Why're we doing this one?" one of the men asked of another.

This fellow worked far less than the others, and seemed fascinated by the thin and flimsy thing he carried around, often laying it out before him. "Because it's marked," was his sole reply.

"Okay," said the first man, shrugging.

As the man approached with the machine, I considered not how unfortunate I was to be facing my mortality. Instead, I chose to spend my last few moments in awe of my offspring, just across the valley. It had matured, bearing offspring of its own. It would carry on the legacy begun by the tree that bore me.

I thought my demise would be a speedy one, as had been the case with the conifers. When the man began to add spikes to his legs, I recalled in trepidation the dismemberment of the maples. Their shape had vexed the men, whereas the conifers had not. As such, the conifers were provided a swift and clean demise. I would not be permitted such an easy fate.

It took the remainder of that afternoon and all of the following day for the men to dismember me. I watched as pieces of myself were fed into yet another machine, only to be turned into tiny pieces, shot out the opposing end. With each limb they removed, I felt a new sorrow. With each limb they removed, I looked upon my offspring with joy.

I refused to permit my life to end in bitterness. When only my trunk remained, I was wearier than I could ever recall having been. My xylem continued to push my lifeblood upward to a vascular system that no longer existed. My phloem had ceased function some time ago. Moisture wept out of each new wound, though with each piece of me the men took it diminished.

When my trunk was detached, a great deal of my waning perception went with it. All that remained was my taproot, and a stump. I found it difficult to cling to life. A tiredness unlike any that the fall had ever brought with it enveloped what was left of me. I was aware that the men were segmenting my trunk and major limbs next to me. I was aware that my stump was being ground down at the same moment. But I no longer concerned myself with the doings of men. Instead, I gave a final offering of thanks. A thanks to my parent for producing me. A thanks to the squirrel for enabling my sprout. A thanks to the earth for sustaining me. A thanks to the sun for the life-giving energy and hope that it had so often provided.

I contemplated my offspring, one last time, and gave a final thanks to them. A thanks for having permitted me to carry on, even in a world where I would exist no more.

That was my life. It was a miracle, and a wonder, and a triumph. This was my final thought as I fell into my final slumber.

ABOUT THE CONTRIBUTORS

Heath D. Alberts is the author of four novels ('Terminal Beginning', 'Last Rights', 'Photographic Memory' & 'Not on the List'), a marketing and business strategy guide geared toward cottage & small business owners ('Guerrilla Business 2.0'), a collection of short stories ('A Twist of Fate'), has co-authored an addiction recovery memoir ('Dave's Not Here'), and was a contributor to the 'Secret Rockford' book project. He is a regular contributor to, and administrator of, The Rockford Blog (author of the 'Remembrances of Pauline Avenue' & 'Rockford's Own' series'), as well as the co-founder of Digital Ninjas Media, Inc. A native of Rockford, Illinois, and an avid collector of rare & first-edition books, he now resides in Rockton, Illinois with his wife, Wanda, and his malicious cat.

Ernie Fuhr is a high school teacher in Rockford Public Schools, having lived and worked here since 1991. Mr. Fuhr is originally from Rock Island County, Illinois, where he grew up on his family's farm. He was formally educated at Western Illinois University with a degree in History & Political Science. He also holds a principal's certificate, having earned a Master's degree in Education Administration from Northern Illinois. Ernie has an inquisitive mind and a lifelong passion for reading, writing, and researching. He recently authored a biography of Rockford baseball player Hal Carlson, which was published in the book 'Winning On the North Side: The 1929 Chicago Cubs'. His work has also appeared in local literary anthologies, 'Secret Rockford', and 'The Rockford Review'. Ernie and his wife Stephanie are the proud parents of two tuxedo cats.

Krystina Fuhrer is a freelance artist based in Janesville, Wisconsin. She achieved her Associate's degree from UW Rock County and is pursuing her Bachelor's at UW Whitewater. Though this is her first publication, her works have been shown in several small and local shows, as well as a number of juried shows.

Casandra Goldsmith has been writing in one form or another since she was very young. She has lived in the Rockford area for the past fifteen years. Casandra works in the health care and wellness industry as a Licensed Massage Therapist, and lives with her husband and their two dogs.

Tim Hughes has published opinion pieces, letters to the editor, and music reviews in the Rockford Register Star, the Rock River Times, and the Chicago Tribune. He has written reviews for the Rockford Symphony Orchestra, is the author of a self-published book of poetry, and a children's book 'Spanky: the Cat Who Loved Christmas', which was a publisher's choice selection two years in a row at the American Library Association's national convention.

Jeremy Klonicki is a mixed-media artist who lives and works in Rockford. He is the owner of MainfraiM, a custom framing, lighting, and design company, and Fraim and Mortar, a collaborative artist studio based in Rockford. Jeremy's wide range of work including photography, lighting, and sculpture has been featured in individual and collective shows throughout the Midwest. When he's not creating in the studio he can be found experimenting in vegetarian cuisine at home with his wife and daughter. You can visit him at www.mainfraim.com.

Kathi Kresol has been researching Rockford's past for over a decade. She shares these fascinating stories through her column 'Voices from the Grave' in the Rock River Times and also through her business, Haunted Rockford. Besides researching, writing, and organizing events, Kathi gives presentation all over Illinois on aspects of Rockford History including Ghastly Crimes and Ghostly Encounters, Haunted Boone County, Haunted Winnebago County, and Rockford's Hidden History. Kathi is always honored to be able to tell the tales of the families who made Rockford their home.

Jason Leviskas is a lifelong Winnebago County resident. He graduated from Rockford Christian High School, and went on to receive a four-year degree from Rockford College, majoring in Political Science, with minors in Business Administration and Classical Civilizations. He is currently working in the government sector, and in his free time enjoys consulting on political campaigns. He has always loved writing; putting original thoughts of the heart and mind on paper. He considers himself a novice poet, philosopher, photographer, and has even been known to write a good love letter in moments of desire.

"May we all get so lucky as to come across an 'Octane Girl'."

Bart 'Zethen' Luhman found a passion for writing after writing his first poem in high school. For 15 years, he continued writing and collecting his poems to eventually release them in his first poetry collection. He is a member and contributor to the website AllPoetry.com. His two poetry collections, 'The Road to Nowhere' and 'Return to Flight' are published by Digital Ninjas Media, Inc.

Jenny Mathews is an artist, mother, teacher, and blogger. She's written for Houston Chronicle, Zombie Logic Press, and has kept a blog, 'Bombadee's Garden', for almost ten years. She's illustrated children's books, run a theater spotlight, been a courtroom sketch artist, played a zombie extra, skated roller derby, been the first lady of a small town, and still considers the most exciting thing she's ever done to be raising children. She is proud to be from, and currently living in, Rockford.

Terry Stolz is currently a Master's Candidate in the Written Communication Program at National Louis University (degree to be conferred December 2015). Mr. Stolz's scholastic achievements include National Louis University's nomination to the Who's Who of Among Students in American Universities and Colleges. Mr. Stolz's folktale 'The Bear and The Hare', and his poem 'Blindman' have been selected by the Mosaic Publication Committee for inclusion in the 2015 MSWC literary anthology. Four of Terry's Cowboy Poems have been published in the Cowboy Chronicle Magazine. Terry's poetry has also been published in The Write City Magazine, published by the Chicago Writers Association and its Rockford affiliate In Print. Terry strives to be recognized as an accomplished poet, a respected professor, and published author.

Karna Tecla is the pen name of Rebecca Kojetin, who resides in Rockford, Illinois and began writing in elementary school. Recently retired from teaching, Karna devotes her time to writing and her husband's trucking business. When not writing, Karna plays the piano and violin, experiments with various crafts, travels, and gardens.

A NOTE FROM THE EDITOR

This work took nearly a year to come to fruition. Which isn't all that interesting, until one considers that I had intended for it to take about three months. The reality of the situation was that, as always, I had saddled myself with too many projects at once. Further stymying my effort was the fact that I had never openly requested work from the public, let alone from a single geographic location.

A lot of folks committed to contributing to the work. And I believe that those folks meant well, or truly wished to. But I've learned much in my years in business management, and one of those things is to expect a small ratio of results versus verbal commitments. The stark reality is that, whether we approve or not, life happens. I hope that if this work succeeds we shall hear from those folks again, perhaps for the next installment.

Two individuals without whom this work would not exist are Kathi Kresol and Ernie Fuhr. Their stories, insight, assistance, and fervor for the production of the work were, at times, all that remained to spur me on. Thank you – both of you – most sincerely. You're both amazing individuals, and I'm happy to call you friends.

I also spent some time, in the early stages, picking author & former Rockford Mayoral candidate Michael Kleen's brain. His having produced the 'Secret Rockford' anthology paved the way for this work, and all of us herein owe him a debt of sincere gratitude.

And finally to my wife, for whom the book is dedicated. I can't overemphasize how much time away from my day job is spend writing and editing. I often wonder why she puts up with my zeal, until I realize the simple fact that she loves me. I don't understand why, but she does. And I love her all the more for it.

In closing, know that all errors in editing are to be considered as my own. I edited as I saw fit. However, I am by no means an editorial professional. Writing is more my speed, with editing coming along for the ride as a necessary passenger. As such, please hold no contributor accountable for my errors, omissions, or ineptitude.

About The Typeface

The majority of the typeface within this book is set in Calibri. It was designed by Lucas De Groot, and released in 2007 to maximize the *ClearType* rendering technology developed by *Microsoft*. Calibri is defined as a humanist sans-serif typeface beneath the *Microsoft ClearType* Font Collection. It has recently become the de-facto standard for numerous *Microsoft* applications, replacing Times New Roman and Arial. This year, Comic Sans made a valiant coup attempt against Calibri, which resulted in the deaths of several unnamed authors, whose heads imploded at the very sight of the font itself. No one has seen, nor heard from, it since. It is suspected of hiding out in fourth-rate children's books.